BECOME A FASHION INSIDER

BECOME A
FASHION INSIDER

---

*A modern-day guide to launching and growing a fashion
brand. Earn more and succeed on your own terms.*

BY DESSY TSOLOVA

First Edition December, 2021

ISBN: 978-1-7398230-1-6 (hardback)

ISBN: 978-1-7398230-0-9 (print)

ISBN: 978-1-7398230-2-3 (electronic)

Published by Moda Media Ltd

Editing by Moda Media Ltd

Copyediting by Polished Proofreading

Proofreading by Polished Proofreading

Cover design by Moda Media Ltd

Photography by Sally Dreams Photography

Special discounts for bulk sales are available.

Please contact insider@fashioninsiders.co

To my mother and dear grandmothers, without whose loving patience, I wouldn't have the skills, passion or appreciation for fashion and the crafts.

Note

Throughout the book, there are references made to podcast episodes and interviews with other creative entrepreneurs, helpful books and resources.

You can access those and more at https://fashioninsiders.co/book-bonus

Before you begin to read the book, take the assessment and check where in the growth phase you are at: https://fashioninsiders.co/quiz

Contents

Don't Read This Book

If you picked up this book because you love fashion and can sew, or think you have spotted a gap in the market, can't find what you're looking for or were made to believe in college, that you are so creative and now want to launch your own brand and become wealthy and famous ... then let me stop you right here.

Having a passion for fashion is like an incurable illness and an epic adventure at the same time. It lasts a lifetime, and you cannot get rid of it. It is like an itch that can never be fully scratched. It is something you carry in you forever.

Fashion is not an industry or business like any other. The road to success is not a straight, orderly line paved with sequential clear signs and wins. Quite the contrary, in fact. It is a long and winding road, full of unexpected twists and turns, heart-breaking losses, personal sacrifices, crippling self-doubt and an insane amount of additional skills and knowledge you need to have that no one would have told you about.

But like any adventure, there is something truly valuable at the end awaiting those who work smart and think creatively. There is the exhilarating feeling of euphoria when you see your ideas turn into products that others, besides you, love and buy. There is the feeling of freedom in knowing that your dreams and visions can truly become a reality. There is the sweet smell of success.

And if you are also called to try your hand at entrepreneurship, you should know this too - there is no adventure more challenging or rewarding than going into the world of fashion business entrepreneurship. Starting your own fashion brand is a dream many have, but only a few manage to truly realise. It requires more sacrifice than you can ever imagine.

So, why do it?

Simple: because if you have been bitten by the fashion bug – there is simply no other better way to spend your time, work hard, earn money and be happy doing it.

If this sounds like you, then the fashion business is your calling and if you have to follow it, consider this book your roadmap for your adventure.

In the pages to follow, you will discover what it takes to create, launch and grow a fashion brand in this millennia. You will also see for yourself that becoming a fashion insider is not hard. It requires a mind shift that only you can do.

Contrary to common belief, the most successful fashion entrepreneurs, commercially successful designers and brand owners are not always the best artists, the most creative fashion minds, the most original inventors, nor do they all have a degree in fashion.

Instead, they are creative thinkers, commercially minded artists, smart pragmatists and fearless entrepreneurs who realise that to succeed, you need to masterfully balance perfectionism with compromise. They know how to dream with their feet firmly planted on the ground.

If this sounds like you, I want you to know that I am writing this book for you. I want to help you realise your dreams.

But if you don't recognise yourself so far, if you think that your "creativity" and talent alone will be enough to get you spotted, elevated miraculously, and propelled stratospherically, then please don't turn the page.

I am not saying this to create false curiosity and intrigue. I am serious. Believe me when I say that there are other industries and businesses you can go into where you'll work less, spend your time and money better and get bigger tangible results in a shorter time. Trust me!

Deciding to build a fashion brand is for those truly ready to experience the blood, sweat and tears required. Launching and growing a fashion brand without the right mindset and foundations will consume your days and make you question yourself in ways you didn't know were possible.

So right now, it is your chance to close this book and walk away. If you are happy with your life as it is, keep living it and keep fashion as your hobby. Become a patron of small brands and scratch your fashion itch with your wallet. Enjoy knowing that your passion for fashion can be controlled and does not require you to give up everything in pursuit of being in the creative driving seat.

But if you know, if you are 100 per cent certain that your passion for fashion is a calling, that you want to grow a business out of it and not just have it as a hobby; that you want to draw a salary out of it and there is nothing you want to do more than build a brand...Then buckle up.

By turning this page, you commit to the process of creating something great. Using this book as a guide, you will create a brand that will stand the test of time and defy the statistics.

This is your fashion adventure, and your journey begins now.

How To Use This Book

"Create the highest, grandest vision possible for your life, because you become what
you believe."

Oprah Winfrey

Every fashion brand and business is built on four core pillars: a strong, recognisable, desirable product (or service), a strong market positioning, a profitable business model, and a powerful, constantly evolving mindset.

Signature Product is what all successful brands have. It does not have to be the most innovative, but it needs to somehow be different, better or unique; a product you are proud of and your customers buy because they love it, need it and want it.

Market Positioning is where your brand sits on the market and how it is perceived by the customers. It's a tricky balance brand owners need to strike to ensure they maintain the correct market positioning. If the balance is off, you'll know because your sales will suffer.

Profit Matrix is the least favourite part for most creative entrepreneurs. The hardest to master and the area where most compromises must be made. If you don't know what it would take to or how to get to operating profitably, you won't be in business for long. The time you do spend trying to make it "work" will be stressful and painful. But you can't do without it. Profit is the blood flow for any business.

Each of these three pillars has various moving subparts, which must all be mastered. Everything must work in harmony together, just like a mechanical Swiss watch. Then you have a business that can grow and scale profitably. And the most important secret ingredient that allows for all to operate smoothly is the mindset of the people working in and on the business.

Powerful Mindshift is the superglue and magic pill that is required constantly in any business. In fashion business even more. Most creatives go into business because they want to do more of what they love (i.e. being creative) without realising that in order to get paid, they must learn how to manage, market and sell. Many of these skills do not come easy to most people. Turning a passion and hobby into a business requires constant mind shifts and subconscious reprogramming. Learning how to get out of our own way every day, in every way and clear the path to success is the one constant skill that everyone gets to work on from the very first day to the very last day in business.

"There is a different devil at every level," is a saying often quoted in business. No matter what stage of business you are in, there will be new aspects of a product, market positioning, profit matrix and mind shift that you will need to learn about and get to grips with. As your fashion business grows and evolves, you and the business need the skills required to transition from one level to the next.

Understanding the interdependency of the above pillars is essential. Establishing solid foundations from the start is a must for long term success. As Abraham Lincoln is often quoted to have said: *"If you give me six hours to chop down a tree, I will spend the first four sharpening the ax."* There is no success without planning for it. Nothing lasting is accidental.

And this is where this book comes in. It acts as a trusted and practical guide to those wanting to launch and grow a profitable fashion business. The principles outlined in this book will apply no matter where you are located in the world, your age, or your demographic, regardless of the type of product or service you wish to base your business around.

The book is based on the four core pillars that I have mastered over the many years spent working for luxury fashion brands and what I now teach the many independent up and coming brands I work with. The knowledge behind these four pillars is what is allowing brand owners to think differently and, as a result, create products that are aligned with the brand they are building; price them profitably from the start (or if the profit is slim or non-existent in some cases, have the product contribute to a better overall profit margin); market effectively and grow their brands purposefully.

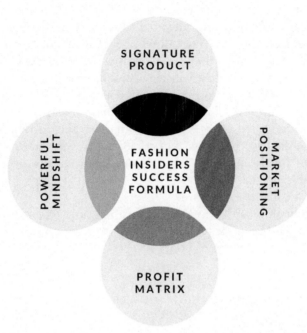

Though the principles and know-how remain the same, how you leverage what you know and where you focus your skills and energy changes from the initial launch stages through to the growth and then scaling phase. That knowledge is ever so nuanced, and it's hard to encapsulate and apply in a prescriptive manner. Every business is different, and it is shaped by different economic and demographic forces. But knowing the core principles is the solid foundation every business will need in order to be able to pivot, evolve and survive no matter what.

This book will give you exactly that. It is a guide to refer to as you evolve your business. You can read it in one go or dip in and out of it as and when you need it. Or you can do both if you are new to the fashion industry.

Don't be too precious with it. Mark and underline the sections you want to easily find and re-read later. Make notes in the margins of the book. Use it as a tool and a mentor, not as a bookend or a paperweight. Research further into some of the ideas I share with you in the book and what is available within your locality.

Throughout the book, you will be guided to additional resources that may be helpful to you, depending on the stage and depth of knowledge you want to acquire (you can find them all at www.fashioninsiders.co/book-bonus). Some of the resources are free and readily available to anyone wishing to deepen their understanding of the fashion industry. The Fashion Insiders & Co podcast is full of informative episodes and interviews with fashion insiders sharing their own wins and challenges. The YouTube channel is full of practical video lessons. Of course, there is a treasure trove of articles over on the blog. You can find links to all via www.fashioninsiders.co

But nothing will help you transform yourself and your business as much as surrounding yourself with other like-minded creative entrepreneurs who, just like you, are building and growing creative businesses. A famous business mentor to many of today's successful businessmen, Jim Rohn, said: *"You are the average of the five people you spend the most time with."*

Think about that for a second.

Entrepreneurship can be lonely. You can choose to do it all alone or not. Wouldn't it be better to choose to do it in the company of others who share the same dreams as you?

Learning together and from each other is the fastest path to success.

You can form or join a group of creatives locally to where you live or be part of a virtual community. Whether you live in a city or desert, it has never been easier to find your people and have the support you need at every stage. I am also creating this through our platform, Fashion Insiders & Co and the Fashion Insiders Business Club.

So let's get going. You've taken the first step by buying this book. Now what?

Easy. **Take the assessment that will help you establish the growth phase you are in: https://fashioninsiders.co/quiz**
Even if you think you know what business stage you're at, still spare five minutes to take the assessment. The personalised overview and recommendations you'll get at the end will be invaluable as to where you need to focus the most in order to Level UP.

After reading the book, you can apply what you have learned alone or you can join the Fashion Insiders community by applying to become a member of the Fashion Insider Business Club. (www.fashioninsiders.co/club)

So let's go. Let's help you become a Fashion Insider.

Introduction

Early Days

Imagine growing up in a grey concrete jungle, in a country where you weren't allowed to travel freely, move house just because you wanted to, or get any news from the outside world. As grim as this may sound, the safety that "not knowing what you don't know" provides comes with unexpected joy and freedom for a small child.

As a child growing up in Sofia (Bulgaria), I was shuffled between my grandmothers, who, like most elder women back then, were experts in sewing, knitting, embroidering, cooking and everything a good housewife was expected to do and be. They dotted on me, the firstborn grandchild and were eager to teach me, as soon as possible, all the womanly skills they had mastered. No wonder at the tender age of three I could already crochet (simple chainlink but still...). It must have been good enough to have my nursery show off my skills to a visiting group of communist government officials.

My mother, was young, beautiful, and loved fashion. She was young when she had her firstborn (me!) and was a little rebellious by the Communist regime rules of the 1970s. She would spend her evenings and weekends tracing patterns, cutting cloth and sewing her own glamorous outfits in defiance to the dismal clothes found in the shops at the time. My father, who had a prestigious job that allowed him foreign travel, was forever tasked with bringing back from his brief foreign travels, fabrics, magazines (containing patterns) and shoes - the one thing my mother wasn't able to make for herself.

Between the women in my family, by the time I was ten, I already knew how to confidently cross stitch embroider, knit, crochet, trace patterns, cut cloth and sew clothes.

As I grew up, so did my interest in art. I spent hours in a quaint city park, where artists gathered to paint together and sell their art. I would stand and watch them draw for hours and hurry back home to practise what I had learned. Getting art lessons was out of the question. Had I wanted to play a sport - any sport - I would have been supported and encouraged. Art, on the other hand? No! A close family relative had taken ten long years to get accepted into the National Academy of Arts in Sofia and then, taken (almost as long) to graduate. He was a gregarious character and a Boheme. As such, he had single-handedly taken up the entire "family quota" for creatives.

Growing up in Communist Bulgaria meant that all good jobs were in state-owned companies. All families aspired to have their kids finish university, get a good stable job and be members of the Communist party. Working alone, as self-employed, was somewhat looked down upon. It got people talking as to why you didn't make the cut. Was it that you couldn't get into university? Perhaps you came from a "less" middle-class family and didn't have the right contacts? Or maybe you weren't up to the party standards?

Connections and bureaucracy were currency in those days. Nothing fast or good ever happened unless you had the "right" contacts.

The fashion industry in the 1980s I grew up in was also state-operated. A small handful of women, well connected undoubtedly, working from an office in the centre of the city oversaw the "design" and "promotion" of everything fashion-related in the whole country. Trends were heavily Russian influenced, or if they somehow made it all the way from the West, they came years late and remained in fashion for way longer than you can imagine possible (remember the 1980s shoulder pads craze... you can still see the remnants of that trend in some parts of Bulgaria).

Most shops had the same limited range of basic clothes and accessories in a few core colours. Anything new and more "fashionable" often sold out before making it out of the storage room. I cannot think or remember any Bulgarian independent fashion brands or designers, though there must have been... surely. If there were any, just like the national pop stars at the time, they were some high ranking party member proteges.

I grew up knowing that somehow, by hook or by crook, the arts, crafts and fashion would be my future. I simply trusted that when the time came, a family member would find the right connection to get me a fashion job. Until then, I had to be a good communist youth party member and get good grades, so I did not embarrass my family and fail to get into university on the first attempt.

Hello London

In the summer of 1989, my father was suddenly sent to work in London, UK. Hello uncensored fashion... Hello Kings Road, Kensington Market and fashion freedom where there are no rules about how to put outfits together. No "tuck your sweater in so you don't catch a cold" advice and "you must match your shoes, belt and bag" style rules. Family pride and society expectations meant that I had to spend four years studying politics, economics and languages before I could finally enrol into a Fashion degree. But that was a small price to pay if I could get into fashion eventually.

Like most fashion students, I worked hard to become a designer. There was no fallback option, as the only other job I knew of was of something called a "buyer." I wasn't sure back then what exactly a "buyer" did, but upon hearing that being good at math was required, that career path was quickly crossed off of the shortlist of possibilities. Math and I were like oil and water, or so I believed at the time.

My first work placement before graduation resulted in my first full-time fashion job. I worked directly with the fashion designer Edina Ronay. Despite her business becoming a casualty of the 1990's recession, all she knew was fashion, and there was no stopping her. She had scaled right back and moved operations to her home. Her tiny team consisted of her, her husband, and a childhood friend. And I became the fourth wheel. To say these first two years of my fashion career were a baptism of fire would be an understatement, but I loved every day I spent working with them. It is during this time that I pretty much learned everything I needed to know (and more!) about the business of fashion.

I helped design collections, called suppliers, ordered trims and materials, called factories and chased production, went in person to quality control and hand-deliver or collect samples and production, assisted in fittings, ironed, picked and packed orders, sewed in labels and mended faulty samples, set up exhibition stands and sold to buyers, processed the faxed orders and did a little bookkeeping occasionally, met with private clients and helped them chose what to buy... even housesat for them when needed. Whatever fashion-related job you can think of, I most probably did it. And for the most part, I loved every single task and job I was asked to do, except for one thing... the pay!

After two years, I walked away from this job and walked into Burberry, armed with two invaluable realisations: fashion was a really badly paid industry (for the most part) and I most definitely did not want to be a fashion designer.

Burberry allowed me to become fully immersed in the creative process, without being the designer. Working closely with manufacturers from all over the world, making luxury accessory products, without being responsible for the production was a dream job. No two days or collections were ever the same. Back in those days, Burberry was not the Burberry we know today. I was responsible for my own mini department (soft accessories) and for generating ideas, thinking up new products, finding suppliers and briefing the factories to create a myriad of samples… in short, I kind of had a creative *carte blanche*, so long as those ideas and products generated sales.

Over the years that followed, I moved from working for one fashion brand to another. With every move, I got better pay, more responsibility, the opportunity to work on more product categories, turn sketches into amazing products, meet new suppliers, visit factories and travel more. Depending on how small the brand was or how senior I became over time, I got involved in every aspect of growing a fashion brand - from the initial creative stages, the number-crunching painful meetings, to marketing, PR, sales and in-store training.

After a while, the desire to design (but not to a dictated price point and a design brief) arose in me, and I ventured into launching my own fine jewellery brand. What did I know about jewellery? Not a lot at that time (except wearing it!) is the answer.

Jewellery was just about the only product category I didn't know much about and it was not in direct competition with my day job. I had no experience in knowing how to make jewellery, but I knew what I wanted and I knew how to work with factories and get them to make what I want. Before I knew it, I worked by day for a luxury leathergoods brand and by night for my own luxury fine jewellery brand. Holidays became "work trips" when I would go to international trade fairs to showcase my brand and travel to oversee my own manufacturing.

And this double act continued for many years until I realised that, as the old proverb goes, you cannot ride two horses at the same time. By the time I stopped actively growing my fine jewellery business, I had left working for mainstream fashion luxury brands and entered the world of entrepreneurship.

The 15+ years spent creating products that generated millions in sales, the countless hours spent in meetings strategising over margins, profit, and collection ranges, all in the name of growing international luxury brands, had given me an incredible insight and experience.

Over the years, I had grown more and more interested in the business side of the fashion industry. It felt like it was time to put this knowledge to good use and create the change I wanted to see in the fashion industry.

Smoke & Mirrors

According to mainstream publications and most online veritable sources, the average business survival rate is 80% in the first year of business, approximately 50% by year five and more than 70% of businesses fail by the end of a decade. While this statistic is not great, I will bet anything that the numbers are even grimmer in fashion. But as you will soon find out, the fashion industry is renowned for being opaque, particularly when it comes to small business statistics. So these and many other facts and figures you may want to know – you won't find. Instead, you will have to learn how to operate on assumptions.

Why are these statistics so dismal? How can fashion be any harder than, say, the food industry, business, or other industry?

The answer is simple.

Smoke and mirrors.

Yes - the fashion industry functions in a vacuum of smoke and mirrors. In fashion, everything is opaque. Despite all the talk of transparency, nothing is transparent. If it was, who would want to buy any of it?

Transparency is not remotely desirable. Transparency will lead to the world being appalled at what cost beauty, luxury, and fashion come at. What good would that be to anyone?

This lack of transparency also means that the industry is highly unregulated and full of people who want to remain part of it at any cost. As a result, there are no rules. There are no manuals and good business books that help creative outsiders become fashion insiders.

The barrier to entry is so low these days, a child practically from the deepest far-flung corner of the world can start a fashion brand and business. No prior knowledge and experience are necessary, and no university degree is required… You don't even need to know how to draw and design to become a designer and start your own fashion brand.

I won't need to give you examples of success stories that drive countless wantrepreneurs to try their hand at it - the examples are all around us. And why not? What have they all got to lose? At best - some money. At worst - more money, their health and maybe even their own sanity. But if they win, the upside is fame, recognition, friends in high places and maybe money.

I'm not writing this book to stop you. On the contrary, I am writing this book to help you.

Unlike the countless "experts" with a few years of fashion experience who overpromise and underdeliver - I want to give you a manual to work from. I want to paint the full picture for you and show you what it takes to launch and grow a successful fashion brand on this side of the millennia.

You can then decide if you still want to pursue your passions or not.

But if you do, at least you have something to work from, refer to and be guided by.

So keep reading.

1

The Ten Fashion Commandments

I f you are reading this book, something tells me that you have more than a passing interest in becoming a fashion insider. This book certainly will help, but before we begin, let me share with you ten nuggets of wisdom I wish I'd known when I first started. It has taken me years to realise, understand and believe in the following harsh truths.

Read and re-read, if you must, the below carefully. If you want to last any meaningful length of time in the fashion industry, let alone experience a faster and less painful journey to success, you need to remember the following:

1. This Is Harder Than You Think

Becoming and succeeding as a fashion entrepreneur is a lot like parenting. I can tell you that it is going to be hard; you can read all the books in the world, like this one, and talk to everyone and anyone who has walked the road you're embarking on, but at the end of the day, you just cannot imagine how difficult and wonderful it will be.

Like any parent, you will worry day in and day out about your business and have sleepless nights. Your business will go through teething problems, and you and the business will both stumble and fall countless times. You will question the ability of others to look after your business and think you know what the best thing for your business is.

Your brand and business will go through various stages of development - infancy, teenage troubles and eventually settle into some sort of stability ... What kind will depend on the series of choices you make along the way.

Just like most parents, when all is said and done, you wouldn't change anything for the world and will do it all over again (hopefully) if you are given another chance.

Luckily for us all, your business is nothing like a child, in as much as you must and need <u>not</u> act emotionally and get attached to anything at any time.

Remember this! You need to have a clear head and think commercially. You need to learn how to "kill your darlings" if needed to succeed. Building a brand and business is harder than you think, but we are tough and can do hard things!

2. Use Your Common Sense At All Times

Common sense is not common at all. This never ceases to amaze me. Even the smartest people, once involved in the fashion industry, somehow stop using their common sense. They don't question "stuff," they should question and accept what is unacceptable, even believe all they are told. As a result, they lose money and make mistakes that could have been easily avoided.

So, whatever you do, hold on tight to your common sense.

Ask questions and sense check everything. If something feels off, trust your gut and at least do some detective work. Have no shame in asking questions until you are certain in something or are willing to take a certain amount of risk, knowing the worst and best-case scenarios.

3. (Always) Follow Your Counter Intuition

I know this may not make much sense given what I just said above but be patient...it will make sense by the end, I promise.

Many may feel like fashion outsiders, but you are an insider of another industry, no doubt. You have skills and knowledge that you have used until now to pay your bills and get to where you are today. Given all you know, you will be correct in thinking that you know marketing, business, accounting ... (insert any other knowledge and life skills you have acquired so far here).

But when it comes to the fashion business, you need to forget what you know. In fact, you need to often ask yourself, "If logic tells me that this (X) is the right way to go about this situation/problem (Y), what would the opposite be? What would a crazy person who doesn't know what I know do?"

Most likely, as crazy as that may seem and feel to you now, the opposite of your intuition - i.e. your counter intuition - will be the right thing to do when it comes to the world of fashion.

Here is an example for you...

If you want to hire a designer, a pattern cutter or a manufacturer to make your product, you will be forgiven for thinking that as long as they work in fashion and have a good reference, they would be a good person to work with.

Wrong! You don't want to work with generalists, trust me. I will explain why later.

You would be wrong to think that any good accountant will advise you and help you grow your fashion business. The fashion industry operates differently from most other industries regarding payment cycles, seasons, trends and more. So don't just hire anyone. Look for someone who has worked with other fashion brands.

Pretty much the same logic follows for anything you can think of.

Also, I know I said above, "listen to your gut," and here I am saying whatever your intuition tells you, do the opposite ... You didn't read wrong, and I didn't make a mistake.

Here is the trick ...

Your gut is an internal feeling. You can feel it in your stomach, in your bones, and you can even smell something that doesn't feel right - correct?

Intuition, on the other hand, is a sense of knowing. When you hear yourself think and say, "*I think this is how it should be*," that's when you know to ask, "*what's the opposite to what I think?*"

Common sense and logic are two different things, and mastering the ability to tell them apart and act accordingly, will serve you well in fashion.

4. There Is No Fashion Police

As I said earlier, there are no rules and regulations in fashion, and nothing set in stone or written as law in any case.

That means that everything is up for negotiation. Everyone is on an equal footing, and yet some are more "equal" than others. Again, this will make more sense as you continue reading the book, but for now, just remember that *there are no rules.*

Having said that, proceed with caution! Always operate from the assumption that you need to always have your affairs in order if there was to be fashion police. Have your own back, document everything, operate above board.

When in need, the rules of other industries can be bent and made use of in fashion by those in "pain," and they'll seek justice.

5. It Is A Long-distance Marathon, Not A Short Race

No matter how hard you work, there is no guarantee that your brand will survive, let alone thrive.

Going into the world of fashion business, for the most part, is not the easiest way to make money. Most "successful" fashion brands you see around - especially the small independent ones - are not what they seem. They may be famous, but they are not cash-rich. Remember … smoke and mirrors!

Let me show you why …

> **It takes at least a year to launch a brand, and only then the hard work begins.**

It takes at least 18 months before potential stockists entertain the thought of spending any short length of time and pay attention to your brand.

It takes at least three years before you (if you are smart and lucky) break even. And before people start referring to your brand as "recently launched," crazy, right?!

Around the 10-year mark, you will be referred to as an *"emerging brand."*

Ok, the above is just an example of what happens to the average brand. Of course, there are exceptions to the rule. But not many, not in fashion anyway. You will be spending money to build your brand and not making a lot back for the most part.

6. The Fashion Industry Is Backward

For all the talk of fashion tech innovation, fast-paced trends, fashion, as an industry, is very backward. "This is how it's done/works/is" is the predominant *modus operandi*. It serves and protects those inside the industry and keeps the challenges outsiders bring at bay by intimidating them and their lack of "knowledge."

In reality, nothing exciting truly is born within the industry. Again, this is broadly speaking, and occasionally there are some exceptions.

Most innovation occurs outside of the fashion industry. Then someone brave and smart brings it in and makes it work for fashion and … Boom! Wow! The fashion industry claims fame and makes it newsworthy.

We can't change that, and that's ok!

But, if you want to be different and in a better place to survive as a brand and fashion entrepreneur, then innovate by looking and learning what is happening outside the fashion industry.

Study the success stories people talk and write about and deconstruct them.

Then use what you've learned, bring it in and disturb the fashion status quo.

Basically - think outside the box at all times.

7. What Goes Around Comes Around

The fashion industry is small. Bad news travels fast.

Keeping it real and being nice to people goes a long way and is the secret sauce to success.

8. Extreme Ownership

Control is an illusion.

You and only YOU are responsible for your own choices, decisions, and actions. It's your business and your money, so you are in charge of everything, success and failure, mistakes and things done right … No one else is.

Even when you delegate and employ people, it is your responsibility to ensure they contribute to the growth of your business and not to its demise.

9. Always Be Curious

The fashion industry can be highly secretive. For one reason or another, many do not like to share - information, knowledge, contacts. In order to keep growing and evolve as a creative and your business, you need to stay curious and accept that if you are going to be in fashion, part of your job would be to be a detective. For as long as you stay curious, you will be in search of one thing or another.

Often it will not be easy to find what you are looking for, and that's when you must ask yourself, "what would Sherlock Holmes do?" Sometimes you'll need to pretend you know less than you do, ask silly questions, use humour or ask for favours and thrall the internet for the vaguest of leads.

In the process of staying curious, you'll find friends, accomplices, partners, inspiration and innovation. And above all, you will create a safety net for yourself with Plan B, C, D and the rest. If you're in the fashion business, you'll need alternative plans all the time.

10. 80/20 Rule

Last but not least, as much as you can, apply the 80/20 rule to everything you do.

Do not chase perfection.

I know, I know … most artists and creatives take forever to complete a work of art because they work on it until it is perfect or hide or destroy it. Luckily, this book is not aimed at artists and perfectionists.

This book is a good fit for creative, entrepreneurial and pragmatic people who love fashion and want to create a fashion brand that exists in the cross-section of passion and profit. If that is you, then embrace the 80/20 rule. For the most part, at least!

You see, 80% perfection is good enough. No one will know what 100% perfection looks like, and getting the data by launching faster and imperfectly is better in most cases.

80% of your sales will come from 20% of your customers.

20% of your collection will be the best sellers and bring in the most money, but you need the 80% regardless.

80% of all that you'll have to do will not be what you love doing (or are best at!), but the 20% is what will drive the business forward.

20% of your business only you will be able to do, the 80% you can, in time, delegate.

And so on. Embrace the rule and use this knowledge strategically to move forward faster.

Being A "Fashion Insider" Is A State Of Mind

So, there you have it.

Those are the ten commandments I have come to believe are foundational knowledge for anyone who wants to make the fashion industry home.

Becoming a fashion insider is not something you need to ask for or wait for permission.

Instead, it is a state of mind. You choose to become one. You choose to BE one. You will always know way more than some people and not enough compared to others. You get to decide if you'll feel like an outsider or an insider.

> **Feeling like you're on the inside comes from understanding how the industry operates, the mentality, and how the different branches of business work.**

This book will give you all that and more. It will take you from the initial major decisions you need to make to start your brand and business, all the way to your "go live" (aka launch) and beyond.

Much of what you are about to learn in the following pages will become the knowledge you will need to have to grow your brand from zero to any number of digits you want your business to turn over.

Everything I will share with you is part of the Fashion Insider Success Formula.

Building a fashion business on the sound foundations of our four pillars of Product, Positioning and Profit and firmly grounding them with the Mindshifts you need to make as an entrepreneur is what sets apart those who succeed from those who do not.

This and more I share, working inside the Fashion Insiders Business Club, which you can find out more about here: www.fashioninsiders.co/club

With all that out of the way, let's get into it.

Let's transform you from feeling like an outsider to a true fashion insider.

2

Fashion Business Basics

"Failing to prepare is preparing to fail."

Benjamin Franklin

Before you start, you need to lay the foundations upon which you will strategically construct your business. I am drawing a reference to architecture because creating a brand and business requires similar steps as building a house.

You need to make a plan, lay the foundations and only then start to build. And you don't start to decorate until you have constructed the building and it is sound and secure to occupy. Depending on the foundations you lay, you can build a shack, a skyscraper and anything in between.

However, what often happens in the world of fashion is the opposite. Using the architectural analogy, what is commonly seen is impatient creatives hastily buying some building materials. They find a few builders to help them put things together (quickly) because they have decided on a reveal date (just like that). They get busy decorating a building site, then they cry that the house they "built" is collapsing, the roof is leaking, and repairs are costly. In some instances, the house has to be demolished completely in order to be rebuilt properly.

I will share more examples of this later. For now, what I want you to understand is that there are no shortcuts when it comes to launching a fashion brand and business.

Your success will depend on a series of choices and decisions you will have to make, over time, and how they stack one on top of the other.

That wobbly house I mentioned above…you won't be building one like that.

You will not be building a brand that resembles a house of cards. That will not happen to you because you are here, reading this book and learning from me and everything I have learned over twenty plus years in the fashion industry. I share the same knowledge with my clients and the *Fashion Insiders Business Club* members who create and enjoy successful fashion brands.

So let's do this properly and start right at the very beginning…

What's In A Name?

Choosing what to call your brand can be an easy or agonising decision. To make it super simple, you have two choices: use your name or give it a name of its own. That can be a word that means something or an acronym.

If you were to follow a certain logic, which I will show you below, then the decision of what to call your brand should not take long and certainly should not make you lose sleep.

When choosing a name for your brand, you need to take into consideration a few key factors.

1. Naming your brand after yourself. Using your name for your business makes it very personal. If you are the sole founder, the creative force behind the brand and plan to also be the face of your brand and use your personality to promote your business, this is a great choice, and it makes perfect sense.

But if you have partners from the start, make sure everyone is on the same page and understands the implications. Naming a brand after one person has a long term impact on the business and everyone involved.

One advantage of using your name is that, more often than not, the name would be easy to register legally, and it would be easier to secure your internet domain for it. Unless you have a popular name, of course.

However, something to bear in mind is that if you use your own name as the name of the business, you must take reasonable measures to ensure that, should anything happen to the business, you can keep the rights to the name for future use. The famous designer Halston, for example, didn't know or was badly advised at the time, but when his company was sold off, he lost the right to use his name on future businesses. He and countless others have learned this lesson the hard way.

2. You can name your brand with a word, a combination of words or letters that make sense or not, the choice is yours. This allows the founders to be less integral to the brand's success and allows a certain amount of anonymity for the founders if they want to remain less visible. Depending on the word you choose, it may be easier or harder to trademark the name and find the domain available for purchase.

Whatever you choose and decide, be mindful of how easy it is to pronounce and remember.

Great brands with hard to pronounce names are not memorable, and ultimately all struggle to gain traction. Brands that have easy to pronounce and memorable names, on the other hand, stand a better chance to be spoken about. Our brains are better equipped to remember certain words and be able to recall them easily at a later point.

When considering the type of name you give your brand, consider your target market and how that would sound to people. In this day and age, when we launch a business, it is online and therefore global. You must ensure your name is not offensive in any of your target markets.

3. Make sure you can trademark the name - i.e. that the name of your choice is available and not already taken by another business. Consult a lawyer or do an online search with the relevant trademark registry office yourself. When registering, make sure you consider the main country territories you want to register for and the main product categories you want to apply this trademark registration for.

Decide on your business name strategically as early as possible. Once the company is formed, and domains and social media handles are registered, it becomes harder to switch.

Start With The End In Mind

Most fashion brands are founded by creatives unaware of the power a fashion brand and business can have.

They rarely think about *what they want to get out of the business* beyond the surface desire to do something they love and get paid for it. Or, in some cases, a desire for fame and fortune. As a result, they never realise their full potential and become trapped in staying small.

So, what if you were to start with the end in mind and work backwards. In fact, I strongly encourage you to do so and make the right choices at the right time.

Here is what I mean …

There are three types of businesses in the world, and you can have any or all of them, depending on what you want. Your outcome desire will dictate the series of choices you make right at the start.

1. Personal Brand

If you named your brand after yourself, then you, as a founder, and the name behind the brand can and should play a pivotal role in your business.

Many fashion brands are named after the creative at the helm of the brand. These founders are usually visible and actively market the brand and products.

They become recognisable, and their customers usually buy the products they create and sell because:

1. They aspire to be like the founder or have the lifestyle and vision the founder is creating.

2. Love what the founder stands for.

3. They trust the person's style, authority and personality.

Here are some examples for you:

Victoria Beckham, Diane Von Furstenberg, Valentino, Dolce & Gabbana, Ralph Lauren, Tom Ford – these and many more are designer brands whose founders we know well. We (can) follow them on social media and love how they look or the world they inhabit and make us dream of. When we buy the products they create and sell, we buy into the dream and vision they create for us. We buy, hoping we look like them, feel like them, and belong to their world.

Issey Miyake, Georgio Armani, Stella McCartney, Eileen Fisher and others like them – we love and buy into their brands because we love what they stand for or the design philosophy they promote.

Personal brands can be powerful because as you build your brand, you are also building the brand of YOU, the person behind the business. That gets you known in wider circles. It can lead to opportunities you never expected, such as consulting, designing for others, becoming a speaker and educator, or even a TV personality.

Also, as a personal brand, you can promote bigger causes and really inspire and create impact. You can champion change and reach out to segments of the population that others struggle to gain access to.

Creating a personal brand makes it harder for copycats to copy like-for-like. They may try to copy your products, but they cannot copy how you promote and sell them and the essence of your brand.

Another point that must not be underestimated, for it can be powerful is that a personal brand cannot be taken away from you since you are the brand.

On the flip side, a personal brand is considered a less desirable investment opportunity to investors. It is harder to sell as a business, and it has an added layer of risk associated.

If you, as a founder, do something silly and ruin your reputation, your brand and business will suffer.

If you are involved in an accident, your business will suffer unless you have ensured and built a team that can operate the business without you for a while.

A personal brand is harder to sell since once sold, the founder will stop being involved; therefore, the loyalty of many customers may be lost.

2. Business Brand

A business brand is just as it sounds. It is a business entity with a team behind it. They specialise in selling certain types of products or services.

People become loyal to the brand because they learn to associate the name with a certain product, quality, and reputation over time.

Just like with the personal brand, the business brand can be a champion for worthy causes and embrace and promote a philosophy of dressing, lifestyle, design ethos … etc.

Such brand examples can be Patagonia (the brand is renowned for its support of sustainability), Nike (sports), Spanx (shape-wear), AllBirds (sustainable athleisure shoes), LV (signature design style), Tiffany (jewellery), and many more.

The lack of brand "face" can be turned into an advantage as a series of well-aligned personalities and celebrities can be used as a promotional tool. Their fame and stardom reach far and beyond what a brand can do on its own. With the help of celebrity endorsements and using them as the brand's face, a brand can build a bigger audience faster, which can be leveraged in many ways.

These businesses are easier to scale and, therefore, have easier investment proportions for investors.

They are also easier to sell as the team behind the business matters, which is "easily" replaceable.

3. Product Brand

These brands are created around a great commercial product. The easiest example to give, though not a fashion brand, is the iPhone. Instantly recognisable product and synonymous with the brand name Apple.

An example from the fashion world would be Allbirds, which have one strong core product they are known for and recognised by. Hunter boots are renowned for their Wellington rubber-made boots; Crocs are synonymous with rubber slip-on shoes ... and so on.

Product brands have many advantages and disadvantages, and often they are the same. They could be considered "risky," for if anything happened to the main core product, the whole business would suffer. But equally, with a strong front running product, the business can become valuable and attractive for acquisition.

What Should You Choose?

The right business type depends on what you want ultimately.

If you are shy and don't want to be "on show" all the time, then perhaps a personal brand is not for you. Having said that, if you want to build a brand slowly and run it in such a way that it stays small but provides enough for you to live off, you have no intention of growing it big and raising external finance, then giving it your name makes sense. People buy from people, after all.

However, if you know that you want to build a brand that is big(ger) and one day you may wish to sell it off for a nice sum of money, then a business brand will be the right choice.

Equally, if you have a strong product that is recognisable and a best seller, a strong personality, and a certain amount of visibility, but your brand does not carry your name as a business name, you can build a brand that has all three business types in one business.

The perfect example to give here is Apple. The business is one of the most successful brands worldwide. Steve Jobs is a name instantly recognisable by millions of people, and their iconic product is the iPhone.

So as you can see, there is no right and wrong choice. The choice is yours to make, depending on what outcome you want. If you don't know at the start, that is ok, and you can choose at a later stage and then re-strategise.

But if you know what you want from the start, it makes it much easier to devise the right strategy for growth and activate it from day one.

Alone vs Partnership

The success of your brand is highly dependent on the people behind the brand. To have commercial success in a business, you need to have a good balance of creativity and business know-how. One cannot succeed in fashion without the other.

Many incredibly talented designers have tried in the past to run a business on their own and perhaps were misguided enough to think that creativity and talent alone was enough to succeed commercially. The fact they are no longer operational is enough to tell you what caused their demise.

So if and when you're deciding to start a fashion brand business alone, be clear on who will balance you out. If you are strong in one area, who will do all the other jobs you are not so great at, don't know much about, or are not interested in doing, because someone has to do these jobs.

Launching a fashion brand is a complex process and takes a lot out of one person. There are many moving parts to take care of and many jobs to be done within the business. Not to mention that as a single founder, you may feel isolated and alone a lot more often than if you had a partner(s).

Many of the most successful fashion brands we know and love today are the product of a successful partnership between creative and business-minded entrepreneurs.

Just like yin and yang, a good partnership has a balance and clear definition of responsibilities. This allows for greater creative freedom as well.

So again, consider the pros and cons and be smart about the choices you make. If you decide that alone is the only way possible, then be realistic about your strengths and weaknesses. Make sure you find ways and people to compensate for your professional shortcomings. Remove any ego and emotion and ask yourself always, "what is best for the business?" Be realistic about what it would take for you to do everything alone. What will it take to bring in help?

If you do have a partner, make sure your responsibilities are clearly defined. Who is growing the business, and how? Ensure your partnership is legally documented and reflects your roles and any initial investment brought in.

Business Structure

Having a proper business structure is important. Some creatives may start alone and evolve gradually. Others may know from the outset that they want to be a company. Choosing the right business structure type is not something that is set in stone. There is some room for you to manoeuvre and evolve the structure as you get going and grow your business.

Sole Trader / Self Employed

To begin with, you may want to start as a Sole Trader or Proprietor of your business. You will need to refer to your national requirements as this may differ from country to country, but by and large, this is the most basic of business setups.

Advantages: As a sole trader, you usually pay no fees to register, and there should be very little red tape for you to be aware of. You are in full control of all business decisions. You only pay tax above a certain amount of income you generate and get to keep all the profits from the business after tax.

Disadvantages: The main drawback to this business structure is that your personal and professional finances are not legally separate. In other words, though you may open a business bank account and do all the necessary to keep your business expenses and revenue separate from your personal outgoings, should the business get into trouble, such as run into debt or is sued by anyone, you personally will be liable to cover any and all costs. So, quite a high level of personal risk is involved in this setup. It is perhaps not the best operational model for any business with high costs and complex operations.

Most creatives who work as designer-makers often choose to register as sole traders. It is simple to manage and cheaper overall to run. But again, the simplicity comes at a certain level of personal financial risk.

Limited Liability Company (LTD/ LLC)

If you want to reduce the personal risk involved in your business, one way would be to register your business as a limited company. This would have to be done via the relevant body in your country. In the UK, this is done really easily via Companies House. In the USA, you need to register via a Registered Agent Service. Depending on where you are located, you can google that information.

Advantages: The main advantage of registering a limited liability company is that, as the name implies, you limit your personal exposure to financial risk. In other words, the company and your personal finances are completely separate. If the business fails (or is sued), you are not at risk of losing your personal assets like home, savings ... etc.

It is also more tax-efficient to be registered as a company, especially when you start to turn over larger amounts of money.

Also, you can allocate shares within your company to yourself and potential partners you may bring in or have from the outset and bring in investors into the business who almost always will require a share allocation as part of their investment.

Last but not least, from the outside looking in, having the status of LLC/LTD makes you look bigger as a brand and more stable, giving confidence to many of the people in the industry you will encounter and be interested in doing business with.

Disadvantages: One downside is that a limited company involves much more administration on a regular basis, which comes at a cost.

To begin with, you will need to contact a certified accountant who can prepare and file your business annual tax return and account reports on your behalf. If and when you reach the threshold for registering for VAT/tax, then they may need to do that for you too.

In short, if you have big plans for your fashion business, sooner or later, you need to register as a company. While you may lose some simplicity and agility, you will gain more stability and a better perception of your business.

Partnerships & Limited Liability Partnerships (LLP)

Without going into too much detail, because it is not that important in fashion and you can easily find more info on the subject, if you did have a partner from the outset and wish to recognise more formally the structure and relationship and a limited company set up for whatever reason didn't work for you, you can formally register your business as a partnership. Just like the above two types, you have a simpler structure and a limited partnership.

As always, there are various business websites and professionals across any country who will be able to advise you what is the best for your situation, business plan and future vision, so make sure you get good advice.

Business Insurance

Business insurance is one of those things that most small brands ignore, often because they genuinely do not know it's needed and only discover they should have had it when they are in crisis or hear a business horror story.

There are a few types of insurance that you can get for your business, depending on what company structure you choose to have. Whether you employ people or not, or if you have a shop or premises where members of the public come to and so on, you may need different types of business insurance.

The best advice right now would be to just remember that you should look into getting insurance if and when you start your business. It is inexpensive and worth having, just in case... you never know! It is there to protect you when needed and when you least expect it and can really do without the extra drama.

Business Tax

This is another area you don't need to know about until you need to know about it, and then it is too late, and everything gets complicated.

So, here are the nuts and bolts of it.

When you first start your business, you will pay personal and business tax (please again consult with the relevant accountants within your country area), but you probably won't have to initially charge tax to your customers. You will only need to register and start charging tax to your product's final price above a certain turnover threshold.

Most fashion entrepreneurs and small start-ups are consumed with keeping prices low and avoid any objections from their potential customers. At the same time, they do not want to compromise on design or materials. They forget to think about what happens when they grow to a point where they legally must register for tax. Thinking about it from the onset means they would have to add extra to factor in the tax deduction in the future. But that would increase the final price to the customer and they fear lead to no sales. So they stick their head in the sand and don't worry about it until they have to worry about it.

But once they do reach that certain level of success in sales, they have to register and add tax to the final sales price. Suddenly, they are faced with the undesired reality of reducing their (most likely not so big) profit margins to pay the due taxes. In the UK and Europe, this is around 20% at present, but that number can vary internationally and across different product categories. (Make sure to check what that is for your country and get professional advice). Alternatively, they would have to increase your prices overnight by that same amount. The latter scenario will not go unnoticed by their customers and most likely will lead to loss of customers and bad comments. It's a bit like being stuck between a rock and a hard place, right?

So do your research, be aware of what comes down the line and plan for it in advance.

If you can, factor in tax from the start into your final retail prices. You will enjoy a bigger profit for a while, and later on, the pain of losing margin will go unnoticed for your customers.

Another idea would be to plan for the time when you will have to start charging tax and work on increasing your profit margins so that when the time comes, you are prepared.

And lastly, you always have the option of keeping your business small and not going over the threshold amount in a single year.

Either way, you have options. The choice is always yours to make. But one thing is for certain, you cannot avoid taxes.

Financing For Growth

I often say to creative entrepreneurs I speak to that launching and growing a fashion brand is like a black hole. No matter how much money you throw into it, it's never enough, and you won't see much return for your money (for a long time at least).

You can, of course, launch and grow a fashion brand on a budget. Many have done it and achieved success. But, whether you're on a budget or not, the fact remains that you need money to launch and grow a fashion brand. Money to pay for materials and execution, promote, market and sell your products, and pay yourself and the people who will help you along the way.

There are many options on the table when it comes to financing your business. In fact, sometimes, it can be confusing and hard to know what the right option is. Broadly speaking, the choices will depend on the stage of business development you are at and the kind of risk you are prepared to take on.

Start–Up Phase: Idea To Launch

When you are first starting out, you may wish to use savings or ask friends and family to help out. This is the most common route for raising the initial finance.

If this is not an option, you can apply for a start-up loan. There are many banks and business organisations supporting start-ups with special schemes and programmes that offer financial support. Most just give you the money, but some also offer additional support like matching you with a mentor, some training, education and so on.

These are great initial sources of money to get you going and help you launch.

Emerging Phase: Pre And Post Launch

Once you are past the initial stages and have a product you believe in, have worked out the manufacture of it, and all the other moving parts that go into the process of building a brand and business, crowdfunding is a good and popular way to raise finance in order to go to market.

Crowdfunding
Platforms like *Kickstarter and Indiegogo* are great for the fashion and creative industry. You can list your product there, and within a short period of time, usually a month, you can get friends and strangers to pre-buy your product. There is very little risk to the customer, as they only part with their money if you manage to raise the full amount of money you set as a goal at the start. The risk is all on you. You only get the money pledged if you manage to meet the financial goal you set out when you launched the crowdfunding campaign.

If you think crowdfunding sounds easy, remind yourself of first commandment: This is harder than you think!

Your crowdfunding campaign success lies in how well you pitch your business and products, how well you structure and prepare in advance the marketing of your campaign, and how much hype you generate during the campaign, especially in the first 24-48 hours. This means that a lot of work goes into it before you even launch the campaign.

The work involves your time and the help of others who will most likely at some point require payment for their work and services. You need to work on collating contacts and building a network of people - friends and industry professionals - who will be willing and able to support you once you launch the campaign. You need their help to generate as much "digital noise" as possible. The purpose of creating hype is that it will bring more eyes to your campaign page.

If you do a good job of the presentation, a small percentage of the visitors will convert to backers (i.e. they will want to buy your product). So, in short, once you launch a crowdfunding campaign, it becomes a numbers game.

There are many intricacies and strategies on how to successfully execute a crowdfunding round of investment. Some companies offer to oversee and manage the process (for a tidy fee, of course). Equally, many articles can be found online and case studies that will allow you to learn and do it by yourself. Either way, two things will remain constant, you will need to put some money into it before you potentially make some, and it will take a lot of your time to do it all with or without help.

So if you decide to go down that route, make sure it is worth it, and you are strategic in how you devise and execute your plan. Here are some key components that you will need to have in place if you want to get the results you need:

1. *You need a great video.* This does not have to be shot professionally, however, do not forget that fashion is all about creating an image. A vision that should awaken a desire and need for what you are selling. It has to communicate a specific emotion and make people either want or need your product. The video also has to communicate who you are, what your brand is about, what's special about your product(s), and where are you going next with your brand. People buy into a vision and the people behind it.

2. *You need an army of people on stand-by.* You need to have at least ten ideal customer-friends or friends of friends who also have at least ten ideal profile customers. They all must be on standby and ready to email everyone they know and promote you, share most if not all of your marketing posts on their social media and help you keep the momentum going, particularly at the crucial first day or two. (If you manage to get enough activity on your page, any pledges and buyer support, you may trigger the algorithms on these platforms, and they could show you support by presenting your campaign to their database. This could be a huge win and get you funded in hours).

Ideally, you will also need to have one influencer who has your ideal target audience. This can be a micro-influencer, but having one helps again with your marketing efforts and helps get your campaign noticed.

You should also create a press list of all the press and media contacts relevant to your niche and target audience, contact them in advance, and see if they can support you by writing something about your campaign. That something has to be published at the time of you running your campaign, not before or after.

Last but not least, get help for you. Think of your mental health and put something in place to ensure you stay sane and don't crash and burn. Get a trusted and able friend or hire someone to project manage this whole project. There will be days when you will be pulled in a thousand directions, when you feel flat and deflated or maybe just need a day off to recharge. Having someone share the workload with you and who can keep the momentum going when you need a moment of rest will make all the difference.

Angel Investors

Depending on how much money you are looking to raise, how commercially viable your business idea is and how good at convincing and selling your vision you are, you may want to look for wealthy individuals who invest small amounts of money in up and coming businesses.

Usually, the amount you can get from an angel investor is greater than what a bank or grand loan could be. Usually, they ask in return for a small stake in your business. Usually, there is no time limit on repaying the investment, but of course, that is up to every individual investor to decide.

There is no limit to how many angel investors you can bring onboard but the more you bring in, the more equity you will part with.

At such an early stage of your business, it is important to maintain a long-term view.

The best way to find these investors is through referral and introduction by someone you may know, word of mouth perhaps. There are a few angel investor networks you can find online. You can also register and list yourself as someone looking for investment.

Grants

Grants typically are financial awards given from organisations to individuals or companies. They usually are given as part of a bigger program and purpose. There are hardly any in the world of fashion, and those that exist tend to be quite limited in terms of who can apply for them.

Still, at least there are some, right?

However, if you are smart, you may find a clever angle to use in order to apply and benefit.

For example, some grants within certain countries are awarded to female creative entrepreneurs of a certain age or ethnic background.

Some focus on particular skills, such as silversmiths or weavers. Some may be age-restricted wishing to support young entrepreneurship.

Then there are larger grants that one can find as part of a bigger community-driven program. Often, these may be international and led by a consortium of organisations and funded by large international entities like the European Union, private or philanthropic foundations, etc. Usually, these centre around projects with high impacts, such as innovation (technical or circular fashion and sustainability innovation) or transparency (increase transparency in the fashion industry through the use of blockchain).

You also have fashion industry grants led by national organisations such as the CFDA in the USA and BFC in the UK, private fashion funds like the LVMH Prize and perhaps others internationally that may not even exist at the time of writing this.

In summary, while there are some grants available, many are specific and restrictive in terms of who can apply but are worth investigating nevertheless.

Amplifying Phase: Grow To Scale Up

Once your brand is established and growing nicely, you might reach a stage where you feel like you are growing too slow and need to accelerate
that growth.

You might reach a point where you have increased demand for your products and need help to finance that growth spurt.

You might be presented with amazing opportunities that, however, require significant investment for participation.

As the saying goes, if you are not growing, you're dying.

If and when you get to this stage, you have a few options.

Bank Credit Facility

If you have managed to grow your business in a way that has created a good credit history for your business, you may apply for a credit facility with your business bank.

This is similar to a bank loan, but instead of having to reapply all the time, you can come to an arrangement with your bank that they give you an open-ended loan. This will allow the borrowing business to take out money over an extended period of time.

Venture Capital

Venture capital (VC) is a form of financing private investors provide to start-up companies and small businesses that they believe have long-term growth potential. The money generally comes from well-off individual and private investors, investment banks, and other financial institutions who pool or ring-fence money into an investment fund.

> **VC investments are typically allocated to small companies with exceptional growth potential or to companies that have grown quickly and appear poised to continue to expand.**

Bringing VC money into your business, as with most financial matters, comes with pros and cons. Without going into great detail, suffice to say that if you get the right VCs on board, the network of contacts and well-connected people they can bring to the table is not to be underestimated.

But on the other hand, they often have aggressive expectations that are not suited to the fashion industry, for the simple fact that most fashion brands do not scale up as fast and as big as other industry businesses. VCs want and expect a fast, big return on their money. Any money they give as investment come with conditions, such as a big chunk of equity in your business, sometimes (depending on the size of the business share they get) they may also negotiate for a seat at the table (i.e. get someone from their team on your business board of directors), have voting rights and a say in how your business is run.

Also, any money they give you comes with a set of charges they levy. All of a sudden, what you thought you would get as an investment is significantly less. So take your time and vet any potential VC investors and protect your business at all costs. Speak to other founders who have had relationships and VCs invest in their businesses and who can first-hand tell you what such investment entails.

Private Equity & Business Share Sell-off
Private Equity (PE) is similar to Venture Capital funding in many ways, except that they are less aggressive in their expectations. Also, PE funds can engage in the buyout of a business, in full or just a share of it, instead of investing money. If and when you reach a stage to seek such serious investment, seek the help of qualified, experienced advisors and proceed with caution.

To round off this section, let me make this clear.

All of the above funding options are available to everyone and every type of brand and business, be it product or service-based. I have tried to organise them to make logical sense according to the three key business growth stages. But as always, there is no rule that says you can only access certain types of funding at certain times.

You can be a start-up and have an amazing idea and know of VCs who may be interested in investing in you and your business right at the start of your business journey.

You may be lucky and get a grand at the start and grow and scale with bank loans and savings later.

There is no one right way to finance your business.

There is only your way. Remember this.

What Investors Are Looking For

Getting funding for a fashion business is easier said than done.

For the most part, fashion is a trend-driven industry and can be highly volatile and unpredictable.

The creativity that fuels success is often built on illusion and lacks the underpinning of sound commercial business foundations.

This often leads to sudden success and then breakdown - not a great promise for investors.

Having said that, fashion is an exciting industry to invest in. The acceleration in technology advancement offers many opportunities to improve, update and disturb the fashion status quo.

So what are investors looking for when considering to part with cash?

To begin with, whether it is friends and family or the bank, any entrepreneur seeking investment should flesh out their idea on paper.

Pitch Deck

A 10-15 slides presentation, commonly referred to as a *pitch deck,* can be an essential tool to outline the idea and business proposition. This should include market research and data to support the opportunity in the market that the entrepreneur is hoping to capitalise on. The pitch deck, broadly speaking, must answer the basic questions a potential investor may have, such as:

• Why should they invest in this brand/business?

• Why should they invest now?

• Why should they invest in you or your team?

• Why should they invest in this market segment?

• Who else is doing what you want to do? What is the competitor landscape like?

• How is your business and product idea different and/or better than your competitors?

• What's in it for them in they chose to invest their money into your brand/business?

Your pitch deck must satisfy the above questions and excite the viewer, even if they are unwilling to invest or are not the right investor. But it must at least leave the reader excited and wanting to know more or eager to tell others about your business.

Business Plan

While a pitch deck may be enough for friends and family to want to support you and invest in your future success, any other more serious investors and lenders will require a lot more information in order to de-risk their investment.

In the first instance, you would be asked to present a *business plan*.

In a few short pages, you must succinctly describe your business idea.

Then, unlike a pitch deck, you'll need to go deeper (yet still concise) and focus on your mission and vision, the competitive landscape, your target market and unique business proposition.

It is always good to include a further SWOT (Strengths, Weaknesses, Opportunities, Threats) analysis and data supporting the viability of your business idea.

Then you should explain how you plan to launch and market your business and show some financial projections to show the potential sales and revenue you think you would be able to generate in 1 to 3 years.

But let me also tell you that even if your business plan was the most amazing and promising, it will mean nothing unless and until you create a great product that people want to buy. (You'll learn more of this in the coming chapters.)

You may also be asked to show when you plan to *break even*, what *percentage of growth* you expect to see year on year and a few more financial questions that a good accountant or business advisor should be able to help you put together.

Aside from the tangible factual information, potential investors will also look at the soft facts, namely, you and your team.

How fit are you as a founder of your business, and why should they invest in you because *a business is only as good as the people in it.*

What knowledge, practical experience, and skills do you have that will support and "ensure" the future success of your business. If you have a team of people, the same will apply to them.

How well do you work as a team, and how well rounded is your team. Are you all doing the same job, or do you have the right people in the right places operationally?

I do not want to bore you nor speculate about the existence of myths and stereotypes within the financial institutions and how those who have the money you need make their decisions, but it is my personal opinion that those myths and stereotypes do exist. You should make an effort to find out what they are and prepare for the occasions when you encounter them. In fact, for this very reason, seek out, as much as possible, investors that align with you as a person and with your business.

Seek out investors who understand the nature of your business and the industry within which you work and have a network of contacts that can help you achieve the growth you want to reach.

Just looking to get investment into your business can be a trap and turn into a nightmare, not to mention that it may even spell the beginning of the end. This is what I call "dumb" money.

"Smart" money, on the other hand, is an investment that comes with unexpected extra benefits and nice-to-have add-ons that help your business thrive. Avoid the former and take your time to find the latter.

The Right Time To Seek Funding

Money is an amplifier, not a magic wand. If you have a bad idea or are not good at execution for whatever reason, money will just amplify that bad idea and get you faster to an unwanted end.

With that in mind, the right time to seek investment is when you know exactly why and for what you need money and what you will do with this money.

When you know based on facts and research that what you want to pour money into is worth it, even if you lost it all, you would not regret it.

When you have a plan on how to make back the money you borrow, then borrow money. Make sure your plan is based on research, strategy and data, not wishing and hoping.

Make sure you know the risks associated with raising finance and what you risk if you were to lose it all.

The right time could be when the potential success is greater than the risk you will take on, and the potential end result justifies that risk.

That is when you will know if the time is right or not.

Of course, raising finance is not a necessity for all businesses. Some brand founders and entrepreneurs are happy to self-fund their business and grow slowly. In that case, seeking an injection of outside cash is not needed. That doesn't mean that you cannot grow a big business. A perfect example of this is Spanx. The founder Sara Blakely is still the sole owner of 100% of her company. Her company is valued at over a billion dollars.

Others, by contrast, like Victoria Beckham's eponymous brand, and many others for that matter, have had millions of dollars poured into them and yet they are not anywhere close to being profitable. On the contrary, many are in serious debt that runs into the millions.

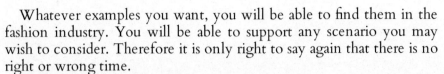

Whatever examples you want, you will be able to find them in the fashion industry. You will be able to support any scenario you may wish to consider. Therefore it is only right to say again that there is no right or wrong time.

Building a fashion brand is a unique journey for everyone. How far you travel and where you get to is based on the series of choices you make and stack one upon another. So choose wisely!

3

Product Market Fit

"You want some good marketing advice? Make stuff
that people
want."

Paul Graham, Founder of Y Combinator

O ne of the biggest causes I see, repeatedly, that lead to struggles, and ultimately business death is the *misalignment* between product and market.

Commonly known as product/market fit, the initial stages are heavy in data research and market analysis. Most creative entrepreneurs, at best, scratch the surface or, at worst, completely skip over this task.

Why? Because some think they know better and already know what they want to do and who their ideal customer is. They think they know what will sell and what the market needs or simply don't know how to do proper research and what that entails.

The main difference between creatives and business entrepreneurs who start a business is that the former operates on a lot of emotion (i.e. I love this, I am my ideal customer, I can't be seen doing that ...) while the latter keeps a clear head and lets the data drive their decision making (the size of the market is X and it is growing or declining by Y% year upon year, so we should do XYZ).

One spends a huge amount of time, effort and money creating and perfecting a wonderful product that often doesn't sell. The other spends less time and money launching a functional, maybe less exciting (not always) product that generates sales but lacks design and passion.

Which one of these two scenarios do you think has more chances of survival? Neither or both is the short answer. Fashion can be unpredictable at the best of times. But neither product will thrive if they are not right for the target market.

If you want to create wonderful products because you want to and don't care if they sell or not, nor have the urgency to turn this, let's be honest "hobby" into a business, then that's fine.

> **But if you want to create a fashion business that generates sales and profits, then you need to do the groundwork and do some deep research.**

The work you will do in this phase will either make you realise this is too hard, that it will require too much effort and money, and that your idea is not as great as you thought it was. Therefore there are better ways to spend your time and money.

Or, you will discover a lot of information that will pave the way for the work you will do after that, better inform your decisions. As a result, you will waste less time, make fewer mistakes and therefore waste less money. Not to mention that you will have an endless amount of information that will help you design better and market to people willing and able to buy your products.

Product

Most fashion brands are founded by creatives, or creative entrepreneurs who either have an idea for a product they think does not exist on the market or spot a gap in the market.

Gaps In The Market

If you spot a gap in the market, that's a great start. These gaps may have existed for a long time or may appear suddenly due to circumstances. Like we just saw with the pandemic. Many businesses were born overnight because of the needs and demand for certain types of products and services the pandemic created.

Before you follow your excitement with action, you must do further research and answer the following questions:

- Is this a new gap in the market, or has it been in existence for a while, and no one has addressed it?
- If this gap has existed for a while, is there a reason why others have not closed it? Has no one else spotted it?
- Is there a problem or pain point associated with this market gap?
- Have others before you tried and failed to "close" it, and if so, why?

Demand for products is driven by desire or need. If there is a gap in the market that seems to have been around for a while, but no one has taken the opportunity to close it, perhaps the desire for this product is not so big? Perhaps the pain point is not so unbearable. Either way, it is important to be clear on why there is a gap in the market and ensure, as much as you can, that you do not waste your time creating a product no one wants or needs.

Painkiller vs Vitamin

One of the first questions to ask yourself when you think of a product that you want to create is:

Is this product going to solve a problem for people, or is it a nice to have product?

This is not a trick question. There is a need and space in the market for both types of products.

Research made by various customer behaviour organisations suggests that people, by and large, are more willing to spend money on moving away from pain than to go towards pleasure.

But we need both, that's for certain!

So, will your product act as a painkiller, aka, solve a problem and alleviate a pain your potential customer has? Or will it be a vitamin, aka, nice to have, it will bring pleasure and joy?

Some products are clearly either one or the other. Many can be both, and that is great.

But being able to articulate and explain why yours is what it is, is most important. Gathering the data to back this up is essential.

Case Study

The recent pandemic created an overnight demand for facemasks.

To begin with, they were hard to find and expensive. Gradually, once people realised they would be wearing them for a while, they began to spend more and look for unusual designs to fit their outfits or personalities.

A US-based company, Rendall Co, was already manufacturing workwear when they saw an opportunity to satisfy the demand for masks. In the course of a year, they made an additional couple of million-dollar revenue simply by manufacturing and selling cloth face masks. Similarly, Bespoke Facemasks was born as a business when the founder - a stay-at-home mum and ex-fashion buyer - began to make masks from vintage fabrics she had at home. The few masks for close family and friends turned into a trickle of international orders and led to corporates placing orders for bespoke masks for private clients and club members.

Sarah Haran Accessories brand, on the other hand, was already successful when the pandemic started. Overnight the demand for her multifunctional, smart work bags would have dried up had she not repositioned her marketing. She quickly moved from problem-solving versatile work bags to focusing on the joy her bags and accessories were bringing to their owners. This resonated with her customers, and the brand boomed at a time when no one was going to work outside of their home and didn't need to worry about fitting anything neatly in a bag.

Different Is Better Than Better

If your idea is of a product that already exists on the market, that doesn't mean you shouldn't do it because someone else already has beat you to it. On the contrary, while there is a competitive advantage to being first-to-market, being second or coming in later can have its own advantages and work in your favour.

The fact that a product exists and sells proves that there is a definite need and market for it. There are people interested in it and willing to buy it. The need for it has been validated.

The opportunity here and now is to see if you can improve on this product or make a variation of it that is different enough, so people would want to buy your product instead of someone else's.

> Improving an existing product with clearly defined demand and target market is a good reason to launch a new product. But you need to make sure that you really are *adding value* to what already exists.

You can do this by improving on the design, functionality or quality of the initial product.

When you improve on quality and functionality, you create a differentiation from the existing product too. This will really come in handy later when you come to market your product.

If you change and improve the design, you also widen the gap between what is new (your product) and what already exists (the competitor product).

By changing all three variables, you have the opportunity to position your product at a different market level and charge more than your competitors, therefore, appealing to an entirely new segment of the target market.

Target Market

Your Niche

Contrary to popular belief, launching into a smaller market is essential, especially when you are a new fashion brand.

I know that logic dictates that the larger the market, the more sales you will make. While this may be the case later on, at the start, the opposite is true.

According to dictionary definitions, a niche is "a specialized segment of the market for a particular kind of product or service."

In other words, it is a segment of people who share similar characteristics that make them ideal prospects to take a particular type of action. In our case, we want them to buy the product we are creating.

The tighter the set of characteristics defined by this niche, the easier it will be to sell to them eventually. Notice I didn't say "find" them. It will not be easy to find a group of people of the same kind. But if you find a few, chances are, you will find more of them too. And if you struggle to find any, all you have to do is relax the criteria a little and make it more inclusive.

Many marketers explain that a niche should be "inch wide and a mile deep". This is a great visualisation of the importance of having a tightly defined niche.

Often when I speak to creatives planning to launch a fashion brand or struggling to grow their fashion business and ask them who their ideal customer is, I hear descriptions like the modern woman, female entrepreneurs, women with sensitive skin, busy working mothers, millennials looking to shop sustainable fashion … etc. … etc.

These are such broad categories that they are not a niche at all. Instead, they can be considered to be "mass" and generic.

If you are launching a brand, for example, with products that are targeting a "modern woman," a "female entrepreneur," a "busy working mother," and "sensitive skin woman," all these "ideal" customers can have a zero shopping budget or be wealthy spenders. They could be located in Europe, the USA or Africa, may be young or older and may or may not be found on social media. Can you see how this is so not helpful to you and your business?

Instead, what needs to happen is to define your target niche further and identify specific needs that will cause these people to buy your product.

For example:

• Women with sensitive skin suffering from eczema/post radiation cure treatments (listen to episode #20 of the Fashion Insiders podcast to hear one designer brand's story).

• Women struggling to find fashionable larger size shoes;

• Women who are a larger size and need sportswear designed for them, with their body shapes in mind (listen to episode #34 of the Fashion Insiders podcast to hear the story of Superfit Hero).;

• Professional women who want affordable luxurious clothing made out of sustainable materials and manufactured transparently and ethically.;

• Professional men who want smart-looking, plain coloured trainers devoid of visible logos and branding.;

• Men and women actively training who are looking for functional designed sportswear clothing, made with innovative materials.;

• Gen Z and Millennials who want we wear to the gym sportswear made in feminine, pastel colours;

• Gen Z and Millennial women who want activewear that looks like daywear when worn outside of the yoga studio or gym.

There are many examples, and if you search online for mission statements of winning brands, you will soon begin to see the clarity with which large brands operate. You will also begin to notice which brands will continue to grow strong and which will, in time, if not yet, lose their way.

> **Because a confused mind always says "no." Clarity is key when it comes to marketing to attract the right fit customer.**

The clearer you are in your target market niche, the easier it will be to find those who fit your ideal client profile. Because you will know where to find them, what drives them internally and externally, what they like and dislike. When you know this and more, you will know where to find them, how to communicate with them, and most importantly, what will make them buy.

One common fear stopping most creative entrepreneurs from committing to a narrow niche is the common belief that this is too limiting and that, as a result, they will run out of customers. What they fail to understand is that this niche doesn't have to stay small forever. It is important to find a narrow niche to begin with, then you can crack it wide open. You can find more of the same niches in other geographical areas. You can add more products to this niche audience (often they will tell you what they want, and you can launch new products to the audience primed to buy). You can relax the niche and widen it. You can do so much, but only once you have started with a tightly defined group of buyers.

You only need to look at the US mega-brand Ralph Lauren to see what is possible.

Remember rule #5 - building a brand is a marathon, and you cannot go from zero to hero in a skip and a hop. You need to do it step by step and gather speed as you go along.

Product / Market Fit

Another extremely common mistake often made by start-up founders and acting as a contributing factor to the failure of many struggling fashion brands is the lack of alignment between the product they have created and want to sell and the market they want to sell to.

In other words, your products (and brand) will only sell when presented to a market that has the interest for this product and the money to purchase it.

Trying to sell a product, no matter how amazing and great to a market that lacks interest, need, or doesn't have the money to buy it, is like trying to squeeze a round peg into a square hole. Impossible!

And yet, so many fashion brand founders and teams overlook this vital prerequisite for business success and fail to address it, let alone fix it.

> **The premise for a successful brand positioning and profitable sales is to find the sweet spot of product/market fit.**

When you know who your ideal client is and you know if your product will solve a problem or give pleasure, you are on your way to figuring out your product/market fit.

Once you know who wants or needs your product, you must make sure they have the money to buy it.

If either of these is not right, you will face challenges.

If your ideal target audience doesn't have the money to buy your products, then you need to either create a new product variation at a cheaper price or look for another target market segment that needs/desires your type of product and can afford it.

If your ideal target market has the money but is not buying your product, then perhaps they don't need it, the desire for it is not strong enough, or maybe there are cheaper competitors, and they don't see the value in spending more on your product.

Can you see how simple this premise can be? Figuring it out is not rocket science either. All you have to do is do some research, present your idea to a group of people you are assuming are the right ideal customers and validate your assumption. We will cover this topic more in-depth shortly.

In the meantime, the third vital component in getting your product/market fit right is knowing the market, which consists of your potential customers and your potential competitors.

Keep An Eye On Your Competitors

Whenever I ask entrepreneurs I speak to (and who are experiencing some challenges) to tell me who their competitors are, I get a mixed list of actual competitors and other brands that are way out of their league. But the reason these competitors are selected usually is based on the logic of product similarity.

A brand that sells a similar product to yours but is cheaper or more expensive, larger or smaller than your brand as a business or not targeting the same customer niche is not necessarily your competitor.

The way I define a "competitor" is simple, I ask the following two questions to find the answers:

1. What brand are your ideal customers spending their money on when buying a product similar to yours but not yours?

2. If your brand didn't exist, where would your ideal customer go and buy a product like yours that will solve their problem or satisfy their desire?

The answers will narrow the list a lot.

Most likely, you will be left with a few names of brands that sell products similar to yours at a comparative price point. Those brands are the real competitors that you need to know of, study well and compete with.

If they are larger in size, more established and on a different price market level, all the others on the list are most likely aspirational competitors. In other words, you may aspire to have a business like theirs one day. Perhaps there are things to watch and learn from them, but most likely nothing to majorly worry about and lose focus over right now.

Once you know your real competitors, it is important to understand how they compare to your product and brand.

This can be done easily by creating an in-depth study of their strengths and weaknesses, looking at their product range, prices, design and product make-up and even how they market their brand and products. This, in turn, will allow you to spot any opportunities that may exist on the market that perhaps you can take advantage of. Or you may spot threats that may create problems for your business.

This analysis is commonly known as SWOT analysis. I suggest you do this for every brand you see as a real competitor and analyse the results individually and collectively.

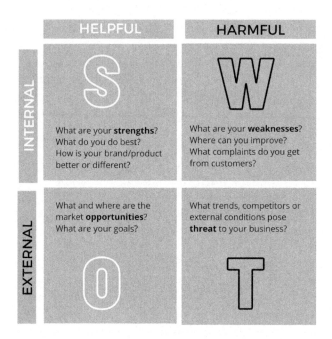

The results will give you invaluable insights and data that will inform your choices regarding product design, pricing and overall brand positioning strategies, of which I will speak more later.

Keeping an eye on your competitors regularly is important as new brands are coming onto the market all the time. You will want to know how the market is changing so you can adapt in good time.

I would suggest you do a competitive market review at least twice a year. Once you get used to this, you will do it without even realising you are doing it.

Minimum Viable Product (MVP) Model

As I alluded to earlier, whatever you learn and create is an assumption until you get strangers to buy your product repeatedly! Nothing is guaranteed to work until then.

Most start-ups design a collection off the back of a few great comments or positive encouragement from friends and family. While this is great to have, it is not to be listened to and acted upon. Friends and family, for the most part, will tell you what you want to hear. Even if they genuinely love what you do, they alone are too narrow of a niche. You cannot build a business relying on friends and family.

Instead, you want to validate the assumption you have made and market your product to complete strangers representing your ideal target market and hopefully make sales.

Because launching a collection takes time, effort and a lot of financial resources, it is best to test the market with a Minimal Viable Product (MVP) offer.

The MVP idea originates from the world of tech. Because launching new apps and digital products is very costly to put together and make work. Tech start-ups usually launch with a very simplistic, watered-down version of the final version product. They test, improve and re-launch and then keep repeating the same process as well as build their brand and business along the way. As a result, you have in almost no time at all massively successful tech businesses that go on to be valued and sell for billions of dollars.

By comparison, fashion brands do the opposite because logic and common sense dictate that this is how you should do it. (But in reality, that is not true. Remember rule #3 - do what's counter-intuitive).

Most launch their brands right out of the gate with a large, costly collection and, almost always, immediately face challenges. Many go on to never recover from the experience. Others limp for a while and shut down eventually. Few survive to tell the tale and share the lessons. Almost no brands exist that enjoy the success SaaS (Software as a Business, examples of which are Lyst, Farfetch, Uber...etc) tech businesses achieve, especially as some achieve this in a few short years.

Ralph Lauren is still privately owned, and if it were to sell, it would sell for billions, but it has been in operation for 50 years now. He might be big and profitable now, but I am sure it took decades before that level of success was achieved.

Burberry, Louis Vuitton and many other luxury brands may successfully sell for billions of dollars, but again, many have been in the making for hundreds of years. If you search online, some of the success stories will be of beauty brands, fashion SaaS brands, and sportswear brands. What they often all have in common is that they are:

• Very clear on who their client is and what function they serve as a brand.

• Have a clear product winner.

• Started with an MVP product or small test range and expanded after countless improvements, all the while selling, tweaking, marketing and nailing their messaging and brand positioning.

Identifying your strongest lead product that will allow you to test your assumptions and product/market fit is an essential part of the path to commercial success. As you are testing your product, you will also be testing your marketing in terms of messaging. All the time, you will be collecting invaluable data that you can react and respond to.

But be careful. Tweaking can become addictive. You must learn not to tweak too much. Only change one variable at a time, so that you can really compare and draw conclusions.

Case Study

Allbirds is renowned as a sustainable shoe brand that makes the "world's most comfortable shoes." They were founded by renewable engineer Joey Zwillinger and footballer Tim Brown in 2016 after spotting a gap in the market for comfortable sports shoes that were plain and devoid of colours and branding. They believed in creating better things in a better way.

While sports shoes were not new and perhaps didn't set out to reinvent the shoe's shape, the brand's values focused firmly on sustainability, meaning that they had to find a way to make a shoe that had the same properties as its competitors yet were completely different. The popular shoes are made of merino wool or eucalyptus tree fibre as opposed to the usual synthetics and provide unparalleled comfort to its users. The founders focused on one shoe design only, and for at least a year, all they did was focus on this one model. They made and sold more than 20+ iterations of the product before they were completely happy with the end product. Only then did they evolve the product design.

You can be successful in many ways, but this is the best way forward if you want commercial success.

The fashion industry is complicated. It has many moving parts that all have to work together and align with each other simultaneously for the outcome to be anywhere close to your expectations. This all takes time and financial resources to execute.

> **The bigger the range you launch with – the more you risk to invest and the longer it will take to execute. The bigger the mistakes you will make and the longer it will take to correct them.**

Money loves speed. Money gives you invaluable validating data, and speed allows you to move faster in an ever-changing (and copying) market.

Once you know what works, you double down on it and make more of it.

If what you thought doesn't work (i.e., you make no or little sales), you ask questions of the "why" variety and find out why it's not working. The data will allow you to either fix what's broken or spot a new idea that may be the winning one. Either way, you are in for a win-win.

Momentum is everything when you are building a brand. Not running out of money, energy, and financial resources to keep going is the name of the game.

Mimicking the winning strategies utilised in the tech world (remember rule #6 - fashion is backward) and applying these to the fashion industry will allow you to manage your money and energy better and build up invaluable momentum.

4

Design & Development

"I don't design clothes. I design dreams."

Ralph Lauren

There is something magical that happens when you start designing and developing your idea into a tangible product.

If you are blessed to have the skills to turn your ideas into products by yourself - by the sheer magic of your hands - then the process is cathartic. It is like meditation. It cuts you off from the outside world and requires you to focus.

If you are acting as a conductor - orchestrating many moving parts to create a finished product - the process will be both frustrating and challenging, but in the end, no less exhilarating than if you made it with your own two hands

The design and development process is the first key step that your business will take over and over again.

Turning ideas into products is part of a never ending cycle.

While a design idea may be sparked off by another idea or be the culmination of experiences and observations, the actual product design is the product of the deeper research you will undertake and the data you collect along the way. That will inform your design ideation and development process to the smallest of details.

Great ideas are not born in a vacuum. Neither is a great design.

A great design communicates visually and has a function (even when it doesn't seem like there is one). A great design binds people together, sets people apart and instigates global change. And then... a great design is nothing if it is left on paper. A great design is nothing if you cannot develop it into a finished product that people need or desire.

Developing Your Idea

Most design ideas are born out of a need for a certain type of product or as a result of research and inspiration. There is no right or wrong. How your ideas come to you is different for everyone. Allowing yourself the freedom to be creative is key.

When I was in fashion college, I studied the history of fashion. I learned a lot about all the big designers from the past. I bought and devoured any and all fashion books and magazines sold at the time in multiple languages. Even in languages I did not speak. I created a fashion encyclopaedia in my head. My visual memory allowed me to quickly reference almost any detail, shape and look I saw or thought of. While this may sound like a great resource to have at one's disposal, in my case, it paralysed me. I felt totally devoid of creativity because I couldn't think of anything new to create.

At the time, I thought working in fashion was about creating "newness." I didn't hear anyone explain, and I certainly didn't come across anyone who wrote about the business side of fashion and its reality. As a result, as soon as I landed my first job, I avoided any design-related tasks. Instead, I threw myself into developing the design idea as soon as someone else created it. It was much later, after many years working in the industry, when I understood how it really works. Only then I felt confident enough to pick up a pencil and a sketchbook and start designing and creating something of my own, by referencing the library of my mind.

While I don't regret for a second not knowing how it worked back then, as it allowed me to develop all the other knowledge and skills I am good at and enjoy doing, here is what I wish someone had told me.

New vs Old

What I wish I knew when I first came into the fashion industry was how to design. That you can, but you don't have to reinvent the wheel or try to create something absolutely new and groundbreaking every time you pick up a pencil. That it's OK to create your version of something that already exists, as long as your version is better or different.

"Fashion has always been a repetition of ideas, but what makes it new is the way you put it together." said the designer Carolina Herrera.

Few designers these days are creative geniuses and able to create and bring to life something that is totally brand new. It looks like 20th-century fashion broke all the norms, challenged all the "rules" that existed and created life-altering changes. So what's there left to invent, and are there any rules worth breaking?

These days anything goes. Nothing is out of bounds. If anything, it looks like society is beginning to create new "rules" that people naturally seek to break.

What is common now and considered a "normal" design process is to take something that already exists and give it a new look. A creative refresh. An update of an existing idea.

If we assume that almost everything has already been invented in terms of product type with meaningful functionality, we either don't have to create anything new or take what we already have and update it by tweaking the design or making it better altogether.

This is how most designers generally tend to work. They take an existing design, update it and make it more relevant to today's aesthetic sensibilities. They take something that already is popular and make it in a different size or material. Or they improve the functionality. Perhaps improve the quality. Or re-design it altogether and improve everything in one go.

While this may sound boring and unimaginative, most of the lead products for successful brands, more often than not, were born via this process. The challenge of solving a problem or working with certain types of raw materials sometimes leads to innovation. Solving design problems and challenges and being constrained in terms of design, functionality, or materials can create something new that paves the way to further newness and reinvention.

Over the last decade or so, the intensified focus on sustainability - taking existing products and customising them or using them to create something new - often referred to as up-cycling or re-cycling - has emerged and become an accepted form of a design process and given its own merit.

Whichever you choose to create, there are no rules. Remember that! They are all credible options available to you and anyone who dares make a start.

If you are lucky enough to create something truly new – commercial or not – it may help you get noticed faster and launch you into the fashion scene.

If you are creative and commercially minded, you will look for what is missing on the market, what can be done better and not waste time reinventing the wheel. There is always room for improvement as life, technology and people's needs and habits change, thus creating new opportunities. The good thing about this model is that it can scale fast and turn into a big business.

And last but not least, if you are on a budget and have strong beliefs around sustainability, big business and fast growth might not be your main goal. Using what already has been made and recycling or upcycling it into something new is a great creative outlet and commercial venture.

You can focus on one of the above or build a hybrid business with a mix of all three. The choice is yours, but don't skip the steps in the process outlined in the previous chapters and the chapters yet to come.

Design Research

Before you begin, your idea would have been born in your mind. Just like a seed, something would have planted it there, and it would have started to grow. That something can be something or anything. There is no right or wrong.

Researching your ideas often is an essential part of the creative process. It allows you to evolve your idea into something new and special, take new creative pathways or make bolder decisions.

Referencing History

The history of fashion is an exciting place to get lost in. Looking through books over the past centuries, one can truly appreciate the changes humanity has gone through and appreciate how much fashion played a big part in it all.

Learning from history allows us to appreciate the present and often predict the future. When you revisit the history of fashion, you will soon notice that it is rather cyclical. Every so often, something groundbreaking or a big trend once upon a time comes back to be "trendy" in a more diluted way. Not always better, but different for sure.

Referencing the rich history of past fashions is a great way to develop new design ideas. Often inspiration can strike in the process and almost literally take over the steering wheel of your research and design process.

If it happens - let it! Allow for your intuition and creativity to take over and lead the way.

Trust that nothing ever happens by coincidence and follow the crumbs of ideas and sketches you'll produce.

You will be surprised where that could lead you to. Almost always, the direction is unexpected, but the results are far better than anticipated.

Inspiration

Many creative ideas originate from a simple flash of inspiration. Inspiration can come in many shapes and forms.

It could be a painting in a book or exhibition you saw, it could be a fabric you touched or a pattern you saw on a passerby. It can be a random detail in an object or an unexpected colour combination. Inspiration can come from a visual, sensory or auditory experience. It can come from a memory or a dream you woke up from. A smell that reminded you of something or someone. The sound of laughter or of the ocean waves.

Inspiration is all around us. Every moment of every day. It is free and available to all of us, regardless of location, age, status and gender. And that is the beauty of it.

When we try so hard to "find" it, that is when we get blocked. Inspiration is like water. It has no shape, and it can be shaped, but it cannot be forced. If you try, something will break.

Inspiration also doesn't belong to anyone, but it belongs to everyone.

Have you noticed how, sometimes, it seems like all the big fashion designers and brands must have had the same idea at the same time? I used to wonder if this inspiration "overlap" was due to some secret insider VIPs meeting, where they pre-agreed on the inspiration they'll use for their next season collection research. Or did they have spies and steal ideas from each other?

The truth lacks such colourful imagination. Since imagination is all around us and as the world gets smaller (thanks to the advancements of technology and travel), we all tap into the same news and global events. As human beings, we are all similarly wired. As creatives, we often are affected by the same beauty and horror surrounding us, and the only thing that sets us apart is how we interpret it creatively.

And that is why allowing inspiration that comes to us and allowing it to flow through us is how magic is created. How good designers have great ideas.

Observation

Observation can be a great starting point for ideas if you are a more right-brained creative entrepreneur - more analytical, logical and someone who finds safety in data.

Observing daily life allows for infinite ideas for products that may not yet exist or ideas about making something better. Observing people and places, rituals, and everyday actions necessitated by needs or desires provides a rich field of research. Add to this the data one can gather from talking to people, asking questions and documenting the results, or reading larger scale conducted reports and summary of findings, and you have endless avenues of ideas to explore and possibilities ahead of you.

Observation is an important part of the research. Most ideas lead to assumptions. Observation allows for this assumption to be developed further and proven accurate or false.

For example, when I had my fine jewellery brand, I observed that almost all of my customers were women buying for themselves. It was very rare that a man bought jewellery from me as a gift. Also, mainstream jewellery retailers always loved my collections but didn't buy anything. The retailers that did buy were small independent boutiques serving a particular niche of clients.

Initially, this observation surprised me but then instantly made sense. My jewellery was not mainstream or of classical design or proportions. It was not small, covered in white diamonds, and as such, it didn't appeal to every type of woman. It wasn't priced in a way that allowed for an impulsive purchase either. The particular design aesthetic I was inspired by and worked with didn't allow my jewellery to be an easy choice for a gift. This observation alone informed my future marketing efforts and liberated me in terms of the creative process. It allowed me to narrow my ideal customer niche further and generate more sales as a result.

As you would have noticed by now, the design process for small or big ideas is fluid. It is ever-changing too. One day it may be a thought that may inspire you; another day, it could be a simple observation. Often, a combination of influences will lead you to a point where your design ideas will crystalise, and you will feel ready to leap into the next step of the creative process.

Design

Years ago, when I was in college, we had a designer visit and give a talk on the design process. I don't remember who he was or the name of his brand, but the one thing I distinctly remember was that he compared the design process to pregnancy. Being young and foolishly dismissive of the value life experience brings, I dismissed his words. I thought he wasn't a good designer. I thought, what does he know about pregnancy being a man? If you are talented and a great designer, you will not need time to think of great ideas. You will have them all the time. I was "certain" of it.

To this day, these words ring in my ears every time I have an idea and do not jump into execution mode immediately. These words remind me that an idea is nothing without the research and development that goes into it until it is ready to be born - one day - into the product or vision you want it to be.

You cannot rush the design process. You can only get better at it over time. You can be better prepared and learn how to execute faster. You can learn how to ask and get help along the way. You can gain confidence and develop your own design signature - a flair if you wish. But you'll find that the one thing that rarely changes is the need to nurture an idea, to the point where it feels you will burst if you don't start sketching or taking steps to bring it into the light of day. And when this time comes, you must start. Even if it doesn't feel like you are ready.

Sketching

Sketching is a great place to start decanting your brain, as I call it. It doesn't have to be pretty or tidy. It doesn't have to be in a book or on paper. You don't even have to know how to draw. Remember - there are no rules! Emptying your mind and creating space for more "new" ideas, solutions, and decisions are just part of the creative process.

Some people sketch a lot, and sketching is a part of their creative thinking process. They think visually. Others may only sketch the final few variations of a design they'll almost certainly be going forward with.

There is no right or wrong. There is only *your way* of the creative process.

Moodboard

Moodboards are physical or digital spaces where the essence of your idea is distilled onto. Once you reach some clarity on your idea and are sure of the direction your design or collection is taking, you may want to document the key sources of inspiration, colours, textures and elements onto a flat board that will act as rail guards while you create.

But let's be real. Because we are all created differently, no one way works for everyone. The design process is more often than not messy.

Moodboards are one of these things that some creatives skip altogether. Some never make a moodboard at all. Others make one after everything is done and completed.

You'll be right to wonder, "why even bother" in that case?

Moodboards are a great communication tool. Not just for you, but for those you work with - your creative team, pattern cutters and manufacturers sometimes, and especially your marketing and PR team members. Moodboards are helpful and useful to have even after the design process is finished.

Modelling

While some may choose to sketch, others may prefer to get stuck into actual experimentation. One of the greatest fashion designers of the past designed by playing with fabric.

Madeleine Vionnet, famous for making the use of bias cut popular in clothing, created her designs by working on a small dummy stand and draping cloth directly on it. Then she would take the mini design, lay it flat and create a pattern from it, which later she would scale up to human size.

Madame Gres, famous for her Grecian inspired long dresses involving meters and meters of fabric, twisted and draped into intricate designs, similarly worked directly with the fabric onto a human model's body.

Jewellers often carve shapes out of wax and play with shapes and ideas until they are ready to make a casting.

Whatever your modelling method of choice, allowing some time for playfulness and experimentation may sometimes seem like an unnecessary luxury. Yet, it is in those playful moments when great ideas are born, or happy accidents happen.

The Design Process

While the development of an idea may be an open-ended process, and it can take as much or as little time you have or allow for it to take, the design process is more formulaic. Or rather, it can be boiled down to a formula of sorts that can help guide you to get to the end result faster.

When you first start, the design process may take you longer. But when you launch and start running your brand as a business and choose to present collections at certain times of the year, you will notice that, on average, the design and development process, as a whole, usually takes around 6 months from start to finish.

Let me explain.

Materials or Design First?

In movies and documentaries, we often see creatives sitting at a table, sketching. We are led to believe that the ideas come first, and it all starts with a sketch on paper, then perhaps a beautiful illustration.

In movies - yes. In real life - no!

In real life, the creative process can be messy, in a wonderful kind of way.

The reality is that we are all wired differently. Creativity comes to us all in a myriad of ways. Some may have an idea that comes to them, and then they search for the perfect material, so they bring their vision to life. Others may fall in love with a fabric or a button and create from that starting point. How you get started doesn't matter. What counts is the end result.

The advantage of starting with a design idea first is that you can be free to dream up anything. There are no constraints to your imagination. The challenge comes later when you need to find the right materials and trims to execute it. When you need to find the right people to make this idea into a finished product and when that product must meet a certain price point if it is to be commercial. What often happens in this scenario is that the initial, perhaps bold and crazy idea, little by little, gets evolved into something more commercial and scalable.

The instances where a beautiful sketch is executed exactly as it is drawn, where the cost of materials and end price is of no concern, happens, but often in custom design and couture.

On the other hand, many designers begin the design process with materials. They find fabrics, yarn, leather, or a precious stone and fall in love with the texture, feel, touch, or pattern. They may find trims and decorative touches that bring to the fore a notion of an idea they may have been quietly sitting on subconsciously. Perhaps it was a movie they saw, an exhibition they visited, or a book they read that sowed a seed inside of them. Often starting with the material is easier, in my opinion, as it is easier to control the end cost of the product or the final outcome.

If the material you love is too expensive, it would be best to design something simple and save money in the manufacturing process. An expensive and costly detail, be it a trim or a sewing technique, can again be balanced out by selecting perhaps a cheaper material to use and keeping the design moderately complex.

If you fell in love with a fabric that is surprisingly affordable - depending on the material - there may be an opportunity to design something a bit more "out there," use a lot of fabric and trims and really push the limits of your creative skills.

Sometimes it is possible to use an expensive material sparingly and balance it with other products or materials to avoid losing the commerciality of your designs and overall collection.

Starting to design from the point of view of constraint can lead to beautiful results. When you must create with a certain price point as a target, you cannot pick and use any material. You'll have to think about your manufacturing costs and what final cost you want to sell. All these are constraining factors. While they may feel like killjoy's, in my experience, these constraints sometimes lead to design solutions that can be more original and innovative.

Having constraints often offers unforeseen challenges that lead to great products. Just think of famous artists and how constrained they were financially when they first started, and yet they often created their most important work during these times.

Finally, whichever way you decide to start, it doesn't really matter. Over time, you will get inspired by your senses, own imagination and physical materials. You may have a preferred way of working, but over time you will try everything.

Material Sourcing

When it comes to sourcing your materials, it is essential these days to keep the thought of your products "end of life" at the back of your mind. While this may not be a convenient chain of thought for some, nor lead to desirable choices - if you do want to be a part of the fashion industry of the future - you must try to consider the consequences of your creative endeavours.   If you want to be respected as a brand and seen as giving more than taking, then it is important that you try to do better with every design and collection over time.

While I do not believe that any fashion brand, large or small, can be 100% sustainable, there certainly is a lot that a brand of any size can do. Little by little, you can stack one positive choice and action on top of another and create a positive compound effect over time.

Sourcing raw material is at the core of any design activity. Sourcing good quality materials that will last longer and not disintegrate after a few wears and a couple of washes is a must.

Trying to use as many natural materials as possible that are biodegradable or compostable is best. If you use blends of fibre, try to use as few as possible. Ideally no more than a mix of three.

It is also important to use materials that can be recycled, chemically or mechanically. It means that garments that cannot be worn or repaired can eventually be pulled apart and new materials created from the fibres.

An example of a brand that does this well is Iro Iro, a small designer brand from India that mechanically shreds waste fabric and weaves new fabrics from the shreds and creates new clothing and interior products.

Further information on the chemical recycling of fabrics can be learned from our podcast Episode 22, where Edwina Huang, the founder of fabric and textile waste recycling Phoenxt, shares more in-depth information. (You can find link to this interview and others at www.fashioninsiders.co/book-bonus)

Design Concept

If you are anything like most brands I work with, you will be designing for business purposes and want your brand to be commercially viable and successful. To achieve this outcome, it is important to have an overarching design concept. The "design concept" is the thread by which your products hang united and your brand, over time, becomes recognisable. It is the magic glue holding together the many moving parts.

An effective design concept serves as the foundation upon which the brand is built.

Developing a design concept demands a clear understanding of your product/market fit, your ideal customer, the competitive landscape, the type of problem you are solving, if any and so on.

Depending on the type of brand you are creating, the design concept can be created around two main areas. Visual elements such as colour, pattern, shape and form can be core factors used by designers as a springboard for their ideas and designs. An example of this can be Missoni - the Italian brand that made machine knitted multicolour zig-zag stripe lines iconic and highly recognisable (and copied).

On the other hand, Vans created a highly recognisable brand of shoes by creating slip-on sneakers made out of checkered black and white canvas material.

Functionality and purpose are more intangible but equally powerful concepts around which many successful brands have been created.

Think of Nike, Adidas, LuluLemon and many other iconic brands - they all exist because of the need for functional sportswear.

All Birds, too, were born out of the need for a logo-less smart everyday trainer that can be worn to meetings instead of shoes. Its functional design also taps into a higher purpose which is to be made out of sustainable materials.

Diane Von Furstenberg became famous with her wrap dress - a functional everyday dress for every woman. Burberry is famous for its trench coat, which originally was invented to protect soldiers in adverse weather conditions.

Examples of solid design concepts that sit at the core of successful brands are all around us. The concept's design development and execution are so slick that most people are unaware of it.

If you still wonder why having a design concept is important, here is another perspective. While not a prerequisite for success, having it acts as a guardrail for your brand in every sense of the word.

It allows you to keep your creativity in check in order to stay focused and "on brand." It allows for the many hands that are involved in the creation of a winning brand and business to know the common goal and be consistent in communicating the main brand ethos and message.

Staying "on brand" allows for a greater chance to become known for something.

People think of certain brands when they need or desire a product. It allows for brands to stand out from their competitors.

Just imagine if Nike didn't have sports functionality as a core design concept. They could make penny loafers and evening gowns, depending on the designer's whim and fancy. Would you think of Nike when you want reliable running shoes? Would you think of UGG boots if you wanted comfy casual warm boots if they also made rubber flip flops, rain boots and trainers? Neither would you go to Missoni if you wanted a little black dress, right?

As you can see by now, the design concept is necessary. It is the inside knowledge and secret ingredient successful brands rarely speak about.

Once you know your design concept, it often means that you end up using certain types of materials or colours and become recognisable through their use, just like Missoni, UGG boots and many other instantly recognisable brands on the market.

Another way to approach brand building and design is to create multiple products aimed at solving a particular need. For example, when I worked for Smythson - a luxury British leathergoods brand - our design concept was rooted in functionality, particularly aimed at discerning, affluent travellers. The core concept around which we created collections was solving a need for our ideal customers. They wanted well-designed luxury products that helped them be more organised. It didn't stop the vast majority of our customers who weren't seasoned travellers or business professionals from buying the products we offered. In fact, many products were bought for everyday use. Even then, customers loved the thought that went into the design of every product. They loved how the product made them feel every time they used it. Though we used some materials that were considered core materials, the secret to the success of the Smythson brand was the subtle evolution of the design. We didn't reinvent the wheel season after season. We presented the same winning products in new materials or slightly updated the design.

Design Signature

Another "secret" design element that plays a contributing factor to successful fashion brands is the presence of a "design signature."

For many brands, the logo may evolve into being just that, an instantly recognisable design element that lets the world or those in the know recognise the product. Think of the Nike swoosh, the Gucci interlocking "G" or the Chanel interlocking letter "C" logos.

As I write this, my father is wearing a black polo T-shirt that is as ubiquitous as a black t-shirt can be, except I recognise the crocodile logo subtly embroidered at the front of it and know it is Lacoste. A friend I met yesterday wore black heeled shoes that could have been made by any brand, but their red sole told me that they were Laboutin's.

The same can be said for the Louis Vuitton diamond-shaped signature design seen across their accessories and often used outside and inside their products. The Burberry check, the Missoni multicoloured zig-zag stripe, the Cartier screw motif on their iconic bracelets, Chanel's camellia flower motif and countless other examples of design signature elements.

Not all brands are lucky to have a strong logo, colour or patterns that can evolve into a "signifier," i.e. a signature design element. Some have to work harder than others to establish such details as instantly recognisable.

Can you be successful without one? Sure! Of course you can. But if you stumbled upon one or strategically designed and embedded one into the minds of your customers, your brand becomes that little bit more desirable, recognisable and stands out from your current and future competitors.

Different Is Better Than "Better"

I mentioned earlier that when I worked for Smythson, Burberry or other large brands, I quickly noticed that we did not reinvent the wheel, which was in stark contrast to smaller brands. We knew what worked and sold well, what customers loved and just made more of it.

When we introduced new collections or added new products to existing ranges, often they were not some amazing, new innovative designs that were patent worthy. On the contrary, we often took what someone else was doing and had great success and made our version of it better or different.

I will never forget day one of my new job at Burberry as a product developer on the accessories team. Coming from a small brand where we survived by constantly creating new products that would catch the attention of buyers and the press, I arrived at an empty desk that had a small magazine cut-out and a yellow post-it note left for me to find. The image showed an "it" model at the time, carrying her newborn baby in a sheepskin leather carrier made by Gucci. The yellow post-it note said something along the lines of "... we need our version asap."

I was stunned. I thought every product Burberry and all the large brands created was a brand new idea. That they had teams and teams of designers whose job was to come up with new unseen ideas.

In less than a minute that day, I learned one of the most invaluable lessons in all of my fashion career. Successful brands focus on creating commercially proven products better or differently. Of course, they also innovate and create "new" products and designs, but not all the time. That is exhausting, risky and impossible to do. And it requires ample development time and budget and the added effort to ensure it sells, or you'll watch it fail.

Taking something that is already proven to sell, liked, needed or desired is another proposition altogether. It saves on development time (that sometimes can take months and years even to finalise) on finances and resources. Above all, it often means it is tested and proven commercially viable. Overall the risk is significantly lowered.

On the other hand, small brands often make the mistake of thinking that they need to constantly create newness. Every season they spend resources and money they have a short supply of on trying to create something new and newsworthy. They often fail to see the amount of unnecessary work they create for themselves, which often leads to overwhelm and exhaustion. They struggle to create momentum and see any significant returns on their investment.

Of course, that is not to say that you should not come up with new ideas. Of course you have to. But you need to build up your brand strategically and leverage every piece of design, content and intellectual property asset that you create along the way.

If you see something that works, be it your own or an already existing product that could work well within your brand offer, then see if you can improve on it or just make it different. Ideally, you may be able to do both - make it different and better.

Making it different trumps making it better. Without copying, you can take the essence of an existing product and give it your own brand take. Redesigned in your materials and colours, with your design signature touch and made to fit your brand concept. Making it not look like a watered-down version of someone else's product is vitally important. That is why knowing your overarching brand design concept and having a distinguishable design signature element is most helpful.

Collection Planning

When building a fashion brand, it is important to understand the importance of collections and how to structure them. Most struggling brands I see and work with often share the same common problem: the lack of a proper cohesive collection.

One of the main reasons so many retail buyers like emerging brands and yet do not buy their products is the lack of a proper commercially structured collection.

Equally, the reason so many brands struggle and fail to gain traction and grow meaningfully is the lack of understanding of a cohesive collection and how to leverage what they have. Great collections outwardly communicate how well the brand is doing (or not, as often is the case).

Unfortunately, creating a commercial and cohesive collection is something that is not taught and explained. It is one of the things most brands learn along the way.

Despite the many years working for fashion brands, overseeing and being in charge of creating and launching collections, the real lesson came to me via the process of building my own fine jewellery brand.

Years back, there was a well respected US jewellery consultant I followed online. As soon as I had the chance to travel to New York on holiday, I booked a one-on-one consultation with her. I wanted her advice on how to break with my brand into the American market. I firmly believed that my jewellery designs and style were better suited to the US market than the UK.

By that point, I had amassed multiple collections - a few in silver, but mostly in 18k gold and a few one of a kind pieces.

She took one look at the display I presented her with and promptly began to pull it apart and create one big pile of jewellery to one side. Then smaller groups of jewellery assembled at the other side of the desk we were sitting on.

The single pile she had made, she waved off dismissively towards, and in a straight-talking, non-sugar coated manner of speaking told me it was no good. Not interesting, and not "on brand". Since most of it consisted of the silver collections, which I felt obliged to introduce when the 2007/8 recession started, I quickly agreed with her. My heart was not into designing these collections, and it showed. I never liked silver much and only created them because of some advice I was given by another respected jewellery insider. (What I failed to see at the time was that they had a completely different business model and aesthetic to me, so of course, their advice was based on what they knew and worked for their brand.) As a result, though I invested time and money to create these collections, I never bothered to sell them. When someone took an interest, I noted their selection and never followed up on the order.

Then she proceeded to teach me one of the biggest and most important lessons anyone had taught me in fashion. This lesson was instrumental to the further success I gained in my fashion career.

Fashion Collections Are Like Human Families

What she explained briskly was, in essence, that fashion collections, no matter their size, must look and feel like a family.

Imagine you come from an Armenian family, she said. *For generations, everyone in your family will be petite in size, with dark straight hair and fair skin complexion. When you marry another Armenian, your children will fit in look wise within the already existing family. If you, however, married outside of your culture - to a tall, blonde swede, for instance - your partner will immediately stick out like a sore thumb in family photos. Your children, however, will be a mix of both cultures and stand out less. Over time, as they grow and expand the family with their own partners, the diversity will increase, or the gap will close, and the family will return to looking more alike, how it all started.*

Fashion collections work the same way, she went on. *Regardless of how many products make up a collection, they must look like they belong together. If something stands out, it needs to somehow be related to the rest. As you introduce new products or evolve the collection over time, it needs to look like an evolution took place. Not a complete clear-out and a family swap. There has to be a family tree, of sorts, that makes sense to the outside world - which are the buyers and your existing customers.*

When retail buyers do not buy a brand they like, most likely there is one of two reasons for it - the brand is not right for their market, or the brand is not ready to be bought into.

The first reason is obvious, so I won't spend time elaborating. The second reason is what prevents most brands from getting stocked at the retail stores of their choice.

The collections they present are not cohesive. They are a gathering of individual products grouped together and given a name that binds them.

Retail buyers, members of the press, and marketers whose job will be to market your collection (now or in the future) all want to see and hear the story of your collection. The collection must itself tell a story and possibly reflect the source of inspiration. If you had a moodboard next to your collection display, the common thread must be obvious.

Retail buyers rarely see a collection by a new to them brand and buy it immediately. Usually, they follow the brand for a few seasons and observe carefully.

How does the brand evolve its collections from one collection to another? How well does the brand tell its own story through its designs? How are they evolving from one season to another – is there a flow and a common thread?

When a retail buyer buys into a fashion brand, they invest in the pieces they buy and the brand itself.

They need to present this new brand and collection to their customers and spend time and effort building the brand reputation to their own audience. This doesn't happen in a day. It takes time and resources. So continuity from one collection to another needs to be maintained. Being able to sell a look rather than just one piece is also important.

When a customer comes and buys from a store – be it online or offline – they too would want to be able to buy a look, as opposed to just one piece. If they love what they see, they will look out for your next collection drop. Imagine if the next collection has nothing to do with what they bought already? They will never be back, and you've lost a customer and potential repeat purchases.

Creating a commercially viable and cohesive collection is not hard once you get the logic behind the structure you need to create. Once you understand the reason why collections must be cohesive and how the lack of one can betray your inexperience as a brand, you will never just create products on a whim, band them together and call them a "collection."

One vs Many

When I explain the above to new brands I work with, I am often told they cannot afford to create collections. Or they ask me how big a collection must be, worried about the cost involved. In fact, anytime I speak about collections, the most commonly asked questions are about collection size. I am often told other fashion experts have said a collection should have 6, 9, or 12 pieces.

I have to disagree. There is no set rule. Anyone who tells you a number, in my opinion, has no idea what they are talking about or is not being transparent enough.

A collection can be as small or as large as you want it to be. However, it must make sense to the customer, the buyer, and your brand.

You can have a collection consisting of a few products. You can launch and grow a brand with a single product. You can also create a collection from just one product design.

Let me explain.

When you create a collection consisting of a few product designs, the most important thing is that these designs work together. When displayed, they should look like a family. When a buyer wants to buy into your collection, they should be able to "pull" a look together. You should be able to suggest to them a look to buy that represents your brand well. It would be a shame if a retailer bought one or two of your designs and mixed in a rail with other brands. That is not buying and introducing your brand to their market. They are buying your brand to accessorise another brand and perhaps fill in the gaps in the other brand's range. There is no relationship building here. Is that what you want?

A collection is like a lego set. The pieces need to be able to work together and create something - a "look" in your case. A top and a bottom, a ring, a bracelet and earrings. Even a necklace for someone who wants the full look. A bag can come with a purse and a smaller and larger version of the same design. Or perhaps a tote, hobo and crossbody for the different customer profiles you may cater to. How many designs and styles you add to make a collection is up to you, your financial resources and the type of brand you are creating. There is no set number to follow.

You can easily launch and build a decent-sized business on just one product design if you are just starting out. That is exactly what All Birds did. That is exactly what Crocs did. That is also what UGG boots, Diane Von Furstenberg and many others did. They started with one great design idea, created one product and took it to market.

The clever thing here is that this one product can be turned to many by offering it in different colours, different materials, different design iterations. Aside from the obvious financial advantages associated with focusing all effort on one product, it is also easier to perfect the product/market fit, the market messaging, and brand positioning as a result. It is easier to build a loyal community of customers and fans.

It takes real guts, focus and strength of character to stick to the belief that this is the right thing to do for your brand instead of branching out, adding on, expanding and diluting the offer. Many will tell you to offer a broader range and that you are crazy to just offer one product. You will be forgiven for falling for the "expert advice" and deviating from your plan if focusing on one product and getting it right was your plan. For every suggestion to add more products, there is a multimillion-dollar successful brand to prove them wrong and show you they did it with less at the start.

The last I will say on the matter is: Apple. Just look at Apple and how Steve Jobs built that brand.

Having said all of the above, remember there are no rules. Neither method is right or wrong. Both approaches are commercially viable. Numbers are not as important as cohesiveness and viability. Also, don't forget that to sell it, you need to manufacture it first. The bigger the collection, the more it will cost to produce, so don't forget to assess your collection through that lens too.

Core vs Seasonal

Another aspect that is important to understand and apply in the process of creating commercial and cohesive collections that do not reinvent the wheel is the concept of core vs seasonal collections.

As you grow your brand and launch and sell various collections and products, you will notice which of your products or collections are selling really well. These will become your best sellers. Your best sellers will form your core offering.

Ideally, the core of your offer will be presented in the form of core collections consisting of core products and materials that your customer base likes. Marketing these products always guarantees sales. These winning products and collections are great to attract new clients with.

You may choose to keep some products in the same materials because they simply sell to existing clients. Why remove them from the range if they still generate sales.

You can also add new fabrics and colourways to these core products and collections as seasonal, limited edition ranges. This adds freshness and newness to the range and attracts repeat sales. Think of your favourite white T-shirt. You love it and wear it all the time and have bought it also in black and grey. But imagine for this summer, your favourite brand brings it out in a couple of seasonal, limited edition colours. Will you buy these? Of course! It's a no brainer - you love these T-shirts and live in them as it is, might as well add some new colours. And better buy these now as they might sell out and not be offered again.

Do you see the logic in expanding the offer of your product range in a strategic and less-risky way?

This is not to say that you do not bring out new products and collections. Of course you have to. You must! That is how you keep existing customers and attract the press and new business. But what it is important to understand here is that you do not bring in new collections at the expense of existing best sellers. You do not have to sacrifice one for the other. You need both!

Creating A Collection That Sells

Finally, if you go through the effort to design, develop, and present a collection to the world, it would make sense to ensure the collection sells. That is the ultimate goal, right?

All I've shared with you so far is essential but not enough to ensure that the collection will be a commercial success.

We have established so far that a collection can be small or large. That it should ideally be rooted in a design concept and have a design signature.

We spoke about what makes it cohesive and shoppable.

The last piece of the puzzle you need to be aware of is the pricing.

Price Ladder Triangle

Another reason why new-ish brands struggle with sales is pricing. That is also a reason why retail buyers may not buy into a brand, aside from the reasons mentioned above.

When you create a commercial collection, you need to also factor in the need for various price points.

Having a broad range of price points will allow different types of your ideal customer to buy from your brand. It would also allow you opportunities to get more volume sales as well as create crazy newsworthy products.

As you will see on the triangle below, the logic is simple.

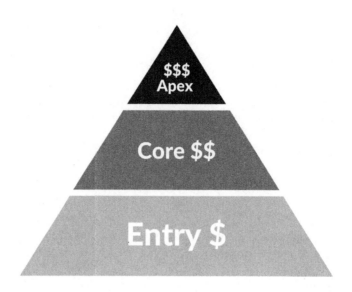

When you design and create a collection, you need to ensure you have **entry price point** products that are easily shoppable. These are ideal pieces for new customers to your brand to buy into and make the first purchase. It allows unsure new customers to make a small commitment and test your brand.

Will you deliver on time or at all? Will the product be as described and of good quality? Will it delight or disappoint? Will it fit? These are all valid first-time buyer objections preventing people from trying out a new brand they come across. Giving them an affordable, no brainer product offer as a taster is a win-win.

An entry price point product is also great for customers to buy as a gift or as an add-on to another purchase.

The **core mid-tier** is your regular price point range where the bulk of your collection pieces should be priced. This is the segment of your collection where the majority of your sales should come from.

The top tier, or **Apex** as it is often referred to, is the top price band for your product offer. These can be one-off pieces that you may never put into mass production but are great press (communicator) pieces. They draw attention to your brand, and people then convert to purchasing from the lower product tiers.

Your most expensive pieces can also be commercial and created with the intent to sell. They will be aimed at your ideal client who has a bigger shopping budget and would like to have something that is less accessible to everyone else. This is where exclusivity comes into play, and exclusivity always comes at a higher price.

When you have a correctly structured collection in terms of pricing options and all else mentioned above, you truly have a commercial collection that is attractive to prospective retail buyers and customers alike.

I will delve deeper into this topic in a later chapter. For now, I just want you to understand the logic of what I have shared so far.

Designing and creating collections is a no brainer for most people. Designing and creating commercially viable collections of products that sell and allow for a brand to grow takes understanding the basics and putting some thought behind every design and piece that makes the final selection.

Collection Size

Another aspect that must be controlled is the size of the collection. The bigger the collection, the more resources you must have in order, not only to develop and sample but also manufacture it.

Designers often perceive bigger collections as a good thing, but it often gives buyers negative signals. It says you are not focused as a brand. The brand leadership team cannot curate and be concise. It potentially signals future financial struggles, as meeting manufacturing minimums may necessitate the cancellation of some products at a later stage in order to manage production.

Even if you did have the resources to develop and manufacture a large collection range, the reality is that not everything will sell. Whatever is left over will become waste. Aside from the fact that unsold leftover stock is a drain on the financial resources of a brand, it is also not good to have from a sustainability point of view.

So, keeping an eye on the collection size throughout the creative phase and during the later stages is essential. The ability to "kill your darlings" is an invaluable skill great designers, brand founders, and commercial teams have up their sleeves. They keep emotions to a minimum and focus on commercial reason and practicality, underpinned by deep knowledge of the target market.

Sustainability

The topic of sustainability is one that is recurring and of great importance. While it may seem like it is a hot topic of late, the truth is the subject of designing more sustainably and in a way that is less wasteful and kind to the future of the environment has been around for years. Fashion is the third-largest polluter globally. Many talk about the issue, few in actual fact, truly do something about it. The competition to be seen as "sustainable" has become a marketing vehicle all brands big and small try to jump on. This has resulted in accusations fired from all sides relating to "greenwashing" and toxic behaviour from sustainability advocates and activists.

I want you to know that while being sustainable is an important part of growing a fashion brand in this millennia, it is also a kind of utopia. It is impossible for anyone to promise, let alone state that they are a "sustainable" brand. They can work towards becoming more sustainable, but no one as yet can be 100% sustainable. Claiming to be one can become harmful to growing your fashion business, in fact. I discuss this in more detail in episode 11 of the Fashion Insiders Podcast, a link to which you can find in the bonus section that comes with this book.

The concept of sustainability is one of the ten principles of Fair Trade outlined by the World Fair Trade Organisation (WFTO). Therefore, fashion brands must work towards a lot more than just caring for the environment to be truly impactful.

Image Source: WFTO Europe

For simplicity, I invite you to think about and work towards being sustainable in two key areas: design and business.

In terms of design – you need to consider how you design from the point of view:

- *How long will your product last?* (This impacts your choice of materials, product quality.)

- *What will happen at the end of the life cycle of your product?* (What will happen to your product once discarded as waste? Can it be chemically or machine recycled? Will it biodegrade or end up in a landfill somewhere and further pollute the planet?)

- *How much waste are you creating as part of your design process?*

- *What is your carbon footprint overall?* (Considering no one can be carbon neutral, the aim is to review your practices and improve incrementally.)

When it comes to the business side of things – sustainability is rarely addressed from that point of view. Yet, if you cannot be sustainable as a business, you cannot have a sustainable brand.

- *Do you work with ethical suppliers and manufacturers?*

- *Do you pay those you employ fairly?*

- *Are you transparent and accountable?*

- *Are you working towards profitability?*

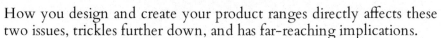

How you design and create your product ranges directly affects these two issues, trickles further down, and has far-reaching implications.

To prove the point, here is what Mark Parker, a long-standing ex-chairman, president and CEO of Nike, said: "*Sustainability at Nike means being laser-focused on evolving our business model to deliver profitable growth while leveraging the efficiencies of lean manufacturing, minimising our environmental impact and using the tools available to us to bring about positive change across our entire supply chain.*"

Working towards sustainability is no longer a choice but a necessity for all brands and creators. Proclaiming "sustainability" is no longer a distinguishing mark and a competitive advantage. On the contrary, it can open you up for criticism. Being transparent and authentic, openly setting goals, working towards them, and keeping your brand accountable is the way forward.

In an industry where smoke and mirrors are the *modus operandi*, honesty and integrity as a brand has become an invaluable badge of honour that customers look out for and reward such brands with their loyalty.

5

Sampling & Manufacturing

"Design is not just what it looks like and feels like.
Design
is how it works."

Steve Jobs, co-founder of Apple, Inc.

One of the most exciting parts of creating and building a brand is the actual development process. Turning a sketch into a finished product and then getting it made and placing it into the hands of your customers. As exciting as this process is, it is in equal measure challenging.

While it may seem deceptively simple initially, your challenges and complexity multiply as you attempt to scale from one (product/sample stage) to many (production/manufacturing processes). The type of challenges and complexity you encounter will be proportionate to the skills you possess.

Like anything in life, development and manufacturing can be as simple or complex as you decide to make it.

I believe in keeping things simple. For the most part, anyway, I want you to know that those creatives that experience big manufacturing problems are the ones who do not know how the industry works, refuse to compromise at times and be practical. It almost feels like some must be masochists not trying harder to learn how to make and keep things simple.

Simplicity in fashion development and manufacturing comes at a price. The price one pays is called "compromise." You have to compromise here and there to preserve your sanity and be able to scale and grow a business. The more complicated your development and manufacturing is, the harder it will be to turn your brand into a successful and profitable business.

Since I have no interest in showing you how to keep a hobby alive, but on the contrary, I want you to create a profitable fashion business, let's push on and dig into the weird and wonderful world of product development and manufacturing.

Sampling

Sampling is an essential process that comes before manufacturing.

After you create on paper, you need to test and develop your design into a 3D product. In the process of testing your idea for construction feasibility, you also test your materials of choice and the fit of the product (on a model ideally representing your ideal customer's shape). The part most forget to test at this stage is the cost of the final product.

In the last chapter, I mentioned the importance of knowing your target retail garment price and developing your design with this in mind. If you create a wonderful product whose manufacturer cost is too high, then you will not be able to sell it, or you will sell it without making any profit.

The goal is to create a product your ideal customer will love and buy. When they buy it, you will ideally cover your costs and be left with profit. That profit, when multiplied over many sales, is what will fuel your business.

If you are not making money from the products you sell, you don't have a business. It is that simple. As the Japanese manufacturing expert Taiichi Ohno said, "Costs do not exist to be calculated. Costs exist to be reduced." In other words, as you are sampling and developing your products, keep an eye on the running costs.

During the sampling process, you will develop your idea from sketch to three-dimensional product. In that process, you may decide to make changes to the design because what you designed doesn't work. Perhaps what you sketched out is too complicated to make and will cost too much. Or maybe what you had in mind doesn't work with the fabric you selected, but you love the fabric more than the initial idea, so you decide to make changes.

This is the stage where you get to experiment and really develop your idea. It's the phase where you prove the concept.

In my experience, it is also in this development phase when, sometimes, mistakes happen that I call "happy accidents." In other words, you didn't intend for something to look or turn out how it did, but you love the result regardless and decide to keep it as if it was intended to be just so.

That is why keeping a flexible outlook is important. It is these very happy accidental mistakes that end up sometimes being the detail or product that makes the difference. So stay creatively open-minded.

Prepare to sample

In order to get sampling your designs, you need to have the following in place:

- Materials
- Pattern
- Maker

There is no right order in gathering these resources, but there is a right execution order which will get you to the finished product. Sometimes finding one component leads to another. Sometimes you reach a dead end, and it feels like you are stuck and can't move forward.

Keeping an adaptable and creatively open mind helps in those moments. Remember, I mentioned earlier in the book that constraints sometimes lead to unexpected breakthroughs. This is one of the places where you may not be able to find something or someone, and you need to reevaluate your initial idea. Perhaps you need to pivot a little in order to be able to move forward.Do it! Don't get stubborn and think, "it's either this way or nothing at all."

The reality of working in fashion and growing a brand is that *your most valued skill will be your ability to problem-solve.*

So, if you ever feel stuck, take a step back and re-evaluate. Find another way, a temporary work-around and push forward. What you need will appear eventually, or you'll be grateful this challenge led you to where you end up going.

Materials

When you start developing your idea, you'll need two types of materials. One is a simple, cheap version of the end material of your choice. The other is the actual material of your choice.

The first, the cheaper version, will be used to make the prototype or initial samples. Ideally, this material will be as close to the real thing as possible in terms of technical properties. In this way, you are not using expensive materials to test your initial design idea and make mistakes. You should not be precious about making mistakes. But if you use expensive materials straight away, you will do just that. Be paralysed by worrying not to make a mistake and ruin your material.

In garment development, a cheap coarse material (that comes in a few thicknesses) is called "calico." This is usually what is used for testing patterns and making initial prototypes. In leather goods, a spongy synthetic fabric-like material is used to simulate leather, which sample makers use.

You don't have to just restrict yourself to using only these materials. You can go to any fabric shop or leather merchant and buy a cheaper material, similar to what you plan to use for the final product and use that to "play" with. Or you can use any leftover materials you might have from past sampling or leftovers from production that cannot be used for future order fulfilment.

Whatever you decide, the idea here is that you use a material that is close enough to be able to simulate the real material and allow you to see how your initial idea will look when turned into a 3D product.

This prototyping process is usually used when you are new to what you are doing (i.e., a start-up new to the fashion development and manufacturing process). The design idea you have in mind is new and requires some testing and experimentation to get it right.

If you are confident and sure of what you are doing and your design, you can skip this part and go straight into using your actual materials and get sampling properly.

Sourcing

To be able to sample, you need materials. Fabrics, leathers, metals, stones, trims...whatever your material of choice, you will need to know what it is, find it and have it on hand in order to move forward.

Back in the day, when I got started in the industry, you would find suppliers at trade fairs and either place an order for what you wanted at the fair or follow up with them later on and buy what you needed.

Today, you have many more options, which is great but, at the same time, confusing.

To find what you are looking for, you'll need to attend fairs, do an online search, contact suppliers directly or look up and talk to agents representing a group of suppliers. Another useful way is to ask for recommendations from other designers, your sample makers, manufacturers and other suppliers. There is no one way to find what you are looking for. Remind yourself of one of the ten commandments that state you need to operate as a detective. Whatever you want, you will be able to find it. You just have to get creative in how you go about looking for it.

In order to keep it simple, you must know what the outcome you are working towards is. That then will reveal what is available to you. Just because something is possible and available to you doesn't mean it is the right choice.

Direct From The Supplier

If you are creating a commercial brand that is based on the traditional fashion business operational model, you'll need to manufacture multiples of any given design. At this point, if you are just starting out, you may not know how much you may want to manufacture. That would depend on the buyer demand if you are wholesaling or the number of products you may want to launch and think you can sell. Regardless of that, what you must consider when sourcing materials is if you will want to be able to repeatedly buy the same materials (for repeat production of a given model in the future) or not. Perhaps if your business model is to sell one-of-a-kind products or limited edition collections, the ability to repeatedly buy the same material may not be of importance to you.

The ideal place to find suppliers to work with is at **trade fairs**. These tend to be seasonal, and these days many have an extensive online database of suppliers, which you can access if you are unable to attend in person.

Those suppliers will (typically) have a type of material or fibre they specialise in. For example, a mill can specialise in the making of lining materials for clothing and leather accessories. You will have a cashmere and cashmere blend woven fabric mill weaving textiles, a cotton mill, a jersey fabric manufacturer, a goat leather tannery, a cowhide tannery, a zip manufacturer, buttons manufacturer and so on.

They will mostly have catalogues of core products that they stock continuously and some seasonal items they may add on to bring in newness and variety to their core range.

Usually, these suppliers will be willing to sell a small amount as sampling to designer brands in order for the designers to test the material and verify it is workable. Sampling often is charged at a premium. In other words, it comes at a slightly higher price.

Aside from the sampling cost, suppliers will also usually quote the actual price should you want to buy bulk for production and their minimum order quantity requirement (MOQ).

In order to ensure that the material of your choice is right for your design, you need to ask the following questions:

• *Do they allow you to buy sampling quantities? (Some suppliers don't. Rarely, but it happens, and it is best to know this in advance).*

• *What is the MOQ required for sampling and the price?*

• *What is the lead-time for delivery, for sampling and for production (the delivery time for both can be different)?*

• *What is the MOQ for production?*

• *What is the price for production?*

• *Is the material you are interested in from their core collection offer or a new seasonal addition? (i.e. can you in the future buy this material again if you want or not?)*

• *If what you like is a new, seasonal offer, what happens if you want to buy more of it at a later date? Can they make it for you again, and at what cost and MOQ?*

• *What if you wanted a special colour that they do not offer in their current colour catalogue? Can they make something bespoke for you, and at what cost, MOQ and lead time?*

So the main things to know when sourcing are the price (per meter/unit), the MOQ and lead time for delivery.

If the price is the right one but the MOQ is huge and you cannot use all of the material, then perhaps this is not the right supplier for you. Try negotiating or keep looking. Or, be creative and ask them if they know anyone who may want to share the MOQ with you? Really, you don't have to settle for "no" every time you hear it. If you want something, there is no harm in trying to get it, even if it means trying out some crazy ideas. (I keep saying this, but the fashion industry is really personable, and if the people you work with or speak to like you, they will try to help you.)

If the MOQ is manageable, but the price per meter/unit is too high, that may not be the right supplier. Or simply look for cheaper alternatives.

If the material of your choice is something you are certain you'll use for other products or many more collections to come, perhaps it is worth buying a larger quantity. But do not forget that you need to have a plan for using it up. And you'll need a place to store it. Otherwise, you may think you are being clever by buying more for a lower price, but unless you convert the material into stock and sell it, your accountant will see things differently. And not in a positive, good for your business sort of way.

Reps & Agents

Many suppliers may not be able to or wish to deal with individual clients themselves. Also, many designers want to see samples and swatches and have someone more local answer all of their questions. For these reasons, many mills and raw material suppliers make sales via a network of agents and brand representatives. These industry professionals are usually responsible for a given geographical area and look after the "clients" that reside within that area. They are the middlemen.

The advantage is that they are local and often have or can request swatches on your behalf. They can meet with you in person and answer all your questions. They have a relationship with the mill and may be best placed to advise, negotiate on your behalf and help should a challenge arise. The small commission they earn is part of the price quoted in any case. Whether you buy through them or not, the raw materials' price includes a small agent's fee.

The best reason to know and meet with agents by far is that agents usually represent more than one supplier.

In that way, they can help you source better, faster and easier by leveraging their network of contacts and knowledge.

The negative is that sometimes if there is a problem, though they may say that they are on your side, in reality, they are on the side of who pays them, and that is the supplier. Their interest is to keep the supplier happy (as they work with the supplier for other clients too) and cannot allow that relationship to suffer.

Third-party supply chain

If you are the type of brand that is making small collections, perhaps limited edition presentations that once sold are not remade again (at least not from the same materials), then you have more and perhaps even more flexible options available to you.

Trade Merchants

These are merchants that deal with raw material suppliers directly. They buy stock from the supplier and sell it to smaller clients.

The prices are usually higher because they commit to buying at the high MOQ quoted by the supplier and then break it up and sell in smaller quantities to those who cannot afford to buy a lot. The less you need, the higher the cost you see.

Sometimes they buy a product line that has been discontinued or buy an end-of-line stock that the supplier wants to get rid of.

While trade merchants are useful to know, their stock is often of the "what you see is what you get" kind. Today it is in stock; tomorrow, it is gone forever. They are not a traditional retail shop. As they only serve the trade. Once you buy, often returns are not accepted. Unless you know what you are looking for and what your criteria for good quality is, you may end up buying something you don't want or can't use.

Online Marketplaces

Since the pandemic, when so many in-person events such as trade fairs were unable to take place, the ability to source materials online has really come a long way.

Most good trade fairs used to have a listing of their exhibitors, but now they also offer the ability to view online catalogues and place orders online with the suppliers.

Privately run marketplaces have also sprung up and offer raw materials ethically sourced from small suppliers that are harder to find on or offline. This is a great way to support smaller suppliers and find more innovative materials, less mass-produced and commonly available.

Last but not least, many suppliers, having suffered through the pandemic and realising the value of having access to their customers, have now developed their own websites into eCommerce portals whereby they directly market and sell their products.

Leftover Stock

If sustainability is a core feature of your brand ethos or you are looking to launch small limited-edition collections, finding and using leftover materials is a great way to create.

These days some online retailers facilitate the selling and buying of leftover stock. Often this stock comes directly from manufacturers or suppliers.

It is also possible to approach their designers and exchange leftover materials. This usually works with smaller brands that are more agile and know and trust each other.

Another way to find leftover stock is to buy from online marketplaces where individuals or small brands may list their leftover materials with the purpose of clearing out their studio space and converting this dead stock into cash.

Last but not least, many large manufacturers often have warehouses full of leftover materials from past client production runs. It is not something they actively promote, yet they are always happy to relieve themselves of these materials. So do talk to your manufacturers and see what they have in stock that perhaps you can take advantage of. It is a win-win for both parties.

Despite all the available options, sourcing materials is not as easy as it may seem. Seeing materials in person, being able to touch and feel the product cannot be replicated online, which creates barriers to purchase.

Sourcing online also exacerbates the challenges created by different languages between buyers and sellers and leads to complications that are easily resolved when people do business face-to-face.

The focus on sustainability and sourcing and using natural materials and particularly innovative new materials also means that many small suppliers fall under the radar and remain inaccessible for small brands lacking knowledge and industry contacts.

This, in turn, means that you must always be sourcing and always allow ample time to procure materials.

The People

The fashion industry operates very much on a person to person network of relationships. Aside from certain areas involving materials, almost everything else involves working and collaborating with people to get your idea realised into a product and then have it brought to the market.

Knowing who to select and work with will undoubtedly be one of the greatest challenges you will encounter – repeatedly – along the way. Creating a network of trusted contractors and "partners" will be one of the main contributing factors to your future success.

Because there is so much competition in some areas and lack in others. With the lack of information and transparency overall and the ego involved, one of the biggest contributors to stress and mistakes is choosing to work with the wrong people. So what makes one person right and another wrong?

Specialist vs Generalists

Fashion is a highly nuanced industry. You will find various moving parts and components within every product category that render one person right and another wrong for the job. Understanding what you need and what makes someone the best person to work on your product is essential.

To make it simple, I will outline the following simple guidelines for anyone who reads this book to follow.

> As a general rule of thumb, *it is vitally important to work with specialists and not generalists.*

When choosing people to work with, be it pattern cutters, manufacturers, suppliers or seamstresses, you need to ensure that they have experience and are skilled in working with the type of product you are creating for the level of market you are working in.

Here are some examples:

A pattern cutter who is experienced in making patterns for soft separates – i.e. blouses, dresses, skirts etc., will not be the best person to work on tailoring or activewear. And vice versa. Pattern cutters become specialised in a category they work with and need to understand how the materials that will be used will behave to accommodate that behaviour via the pattern. The more experienced they are in a garment category, the better and faster they will create patterns that will need minimum alterations later on.

If you took for a seamstress experienced in sewing activewear, she would not be the best choice to make a garment from a delicate fabric. Aside from the fact that she will need a different machine to work on, the seamstress will not be used to working with delicate fabrics and executing with the finesse these fabrics require.

A manufacturer that makes for high street brands would not be the right one to work on a smaller designer brand production order even if they agreed to the terms with the client. They will most likely not be used to the level of detail and quality in execution a designer brand will be looking for.

This continues to be the case for almost every area of the fashion industry. Marketers, copywriters, accountants, designers, garment technologists, models, and photographers all have to be experienced and specialised in working with your type of product or business to get satisfactory results.

The Sample Development Process

Pattern Development

To be able to turn your idea into a 3D product, you will need to have a pattern cut first.

This will usually be done by a pattern cutter. These can be freelancers or be employees of a sampling studio or factory you chose to work with.

As mentioned above, it is important to work with someone who has *proven* experience in working with your type of product and materials of choice.

The more information you give them as part of the brief and your first meeting, the better the outcome will be. The information they need to have should be about the materials you plan to use, the ideal client you have (body shape, etc.), the measurements the garment/product should have, the product's intended use, and any other specificities.

Some pattern cutters cut from the standard blocks they will have; others may drape on the stand. It depends on the design and the pattern cutter you select to work with.

Discussing how they work, the required outcome of the project, what "success" looks like for you as a client and the time they will take to make the pattern are all important factors contributing to the end result and must be discussed and documented to avoid disappointments.

Sample Development

It is important to know the various types of samples used in the industry and why and which type you need to have at various stages, when it comes to sampling.

Also, since they all are chargeable (usually charged at 1.5-2 times the cost of production price, not to mention other development charges many manufacturers add these days), you need to be prepared to meet these costs and allow plenty of time for their development.

Sampling mostly falls under three main categories: development, final and pre-production samples.

Development Samples

To begin with, you may need a rough sample made, often referred to as prototype, toile (in clothing) or salpa (in leatherwoods), that will test the pattern, proportions etc. This is a helpful sample if you are testing something new and not so simple or new to the fashion industry. If you are more experienced or making a variation of a product not that different from others you have made in the past, you may as well go straight on to making the first sample.

Depending on your experience, your manufacturer, your product, etc., the first sample may be your one and only sample and be a final, sign-off sample or the first of many.

How many more samples you make depends entirely on your design, experience as a designer or creative, your manufacturer or sample maker and above all, how many times you change your mind and make alterations.

One of the biggest reasons for multiple samples to be made time after time, which costs money and drives manufacturers crazy and leads to strained relationships, is most creatives' uncanny ability to always want to change something, tweak it, improve etc.

My advice - just don't! Do all you can while designing on paper, and if you have to, make a prototype and play around with it. But when you start sampling with your manufacturer, unless you absolutely have to, do not make changes because you had a better idea and feel like trying out something else. Aim to go from the first sample to the final signed off sample within a couple of sample rounds at most.

Final Samples

The final sample (also often referred to as Final/Sealed/Gold Seal) will be the last sample made that you are completely happy with. This will be the example and benchmark sample product against which future manufacturing will be compared to. It will serve as your pass/fail criteria for future production runs. It will also be based on this sample that your final production costs will be confirmed.

Once you have it ready, you must clearly mark this sample as such and guard it safely.

Depending on your budget and resources, it is a good idea to make more than one of this final sample (unless your past sampling versions are not too bad and can be used) as you would need to use samples of your products for:

• Photography - you need to photograph your product in advance of collection launch in order to be able to create marketing materials and have images for your website.

• Press - if you are actively working on generating press, you will be most likely sending samples for magazine feature photoshoots, for shows, to influencers...etc

• Gifting - depending on the product and your business plan, you may want to have some extra samples made so you can send some to key influencers or members of the press in advance of the launch, so you can start building up some hype.

• Sales - you will need salesman samples if you do trade shows or have agents and reps selling your products.

Pre-production Samples

Once you are ready for production, there may often be some tiny tweaks or reasons for making a pre-production sample (also known as the Top of Pile sample) to ensure that the production will be absolutely correct.

Usually, the most common reason for making a pre-production sample is to test the bulk fabric you received for production.

Or perhaps to confirm that the production team will make the bulk production exactly as the sampling team made the initial samples.

Maybe you didn't end up having a "sealed" final sample earlier, and this pre-production sample will be the final, most perfect version production will follow.

Whatever the reasons, it is good to do one last pre-production sample and approve it before starting bulk production.

Another sample you may request at this point is a full-size set sample. In other words, you ask for all sizes that you will offer for sale to be sampled. This allows you to check the sizing up and down of patterns, though if you spot something at this point, it will be too late to start tweaking and changing. So if you are not sure of any aspects relating to the grading of the patterns into smaller and larger sizes from your original, then you must make sure that this is ironed out at the development stages.

Mastering Manufacturing

I will not beat around the bush and spare you the truth here. It is important that you know the reality and have your eyes open if you want to succeed.

Manufacturing is perhaps the single most challenging and complex area of running a product-based fashion business. It is the most ungrateful job of all and yet, at the same time, the most gratifying one. When it all works out and you get your samples or production just how you wanted them, it feels like Christmas.

No matter what you do, how much you plan and prepare for, you will have some sort of problem with every production run you undertake.

If you don't have problems, you don't have production - it is as simple as that. It has nothing to do with how big or small you are as a business, if you work alone or have a team if you have a great factory to work with or not, if you have money or not.

That is why understanding how manufacturing works, the mindset needed for it, understanding the business basics, and being smart and professional at all times are essential if you are to minimise the challenges you will encounter and get good results. And by good results, I mean getting a product that is fit for purpose and sellable, minimising the wasting of time and money along the way and being able as a result to grow your business.

On the flip side, manufacturing is one of my favourite things to do. The people you will meet along the way and develop good, long term relationships with will be some of the nicest people you will meet in the industry. Getting to know them and their culture is often like finding a second family. Manufacturing is such a personal business that your success or failure is often based on finding, meeting, and forging good relationships with the right people at the right time for you and your business. When you do find them, they will have your back. They will help you more than you can imagine and become part of your team. They will anticipate problems for you and problem solve on your behalf. I often refer to this activity as "moving mountains" because sometimes it really feels like a mountain stands in your way, and you simply do not have the imagination to see how a challenge can be resolved. Then your manufacturer steps in and makes it all right.

It is because of the great manufacturing relationships I have built over the years with so many manufacturers that I have been able to do impossible things - like turn around a large order of belts for a high profile corporate customer in a matter of a few days from confirming the order, to delivery. On that particular occasion, my manufacturer employed extra staff and created a night shift to make it happen. He then packed the finished products in suitcases and flew on the last night flight to London. He crashed on a bench at the airport until the first underground trains started to run and was outside the boutique with his delivery at dawn. Just writing this sounds crazy, but it is all true, and it did happen. I did not beg for any of this - instead, we had each other's back and full trust in each other's capabilities.

I can bore you with countless good and bad manufacturing stories, but I won't. I will let you experience the joy and hardship for yourself, as it is a rite of passage. But I will help you by re-framing the essential knowledge you need to have to navigate the manufacturing process with more ease.

Manufacturing Mindset

First things first, most creatives struggle and waste extraordinary amounts of time, effort, energy, emotions and money along the way, simply because they fail to grasp the mindset of the manufacturing business. So here it is in a nutshell:

• **Manufacturing is a business.** A big business. The people who manufacture and own or work for factories have to make money too. They have to get paid so that they can live their lives just like you. They have to pay bills and pay their employees and other suppliers they work with. They look at their "factory" as a business, just like you will look at your brand as a business. They, too, have hopes and dreams to grow their business, make money, enjoy this money, and leave a legacy. They are no different from you and me.

• **Manufacturing is very much like dating.** Sometimes you meet your "person" early in life and live happily ever after, and sometimes you have to kiss a lot of frogs to find your prince/ss. Sometimes you meet someone and don't think there is anything you have in common, and yet, you get to know them, and they turn out to be THE one. Other times, all the boxes are checked, and on paper, it seems like a match made in heaven, yet it just doesn't work.

This is what the world of manufacturing is like. Finding and working with manufacturers is like a romantic relationship. It takes time to get to know each other, get used to each other, find out what makes the other tick. Above all - to make it work - you both need to have trust, communicate well and compromise at times. When you understand this analogy and apply it to looking and working with a manufacturer, then you will have an easier time finding one and developing a lasting, productive "relationship."

• **Without a great manufacturer by your side, you have no fashion (product) business.** End of story! The manufacturers you work with do not live and breathe so they can serve you and get bullied, emotionally blackmailed, lied to, manipulated and mistreated. They need to be seen as "partners" in the journey of building and growing your brand. They need to be respected as such and recognised for the vital role they play in the process. They are not owned by you (unless you set up your own factory) and work for others too. They are smart business people whose kindness has often been abused so much that they forget they have a heart and may appear detached and cold. So a little respect and kindness go a long, long way. Trust me!

So what does the above mean?

Simply that you need to be respectful and organised. Professional at all times and a good communicator. You need to be kind and look beyond the "business" aspect. Most challenges and failures come as a result of:

Bad organisation - it is your responsibility to make sure you are organised at all times. Exercising extreme ownership across all areas of your business is essential, especially when it comes to manufacturing. The success of your business is all down to you and the choices you make. Being organised is a choice and a habit. If this is not your forte, find someone who is to partner with you. Whichever way you do it, you need to ensure you have all that's required for a smooth manufacturing process on time. That you deliver all of what is expected from you on time. It is also up to you to ensure your factory operates on time (even if they have management in place). Of course, you have to delegate and allow people to be responsible, but factories also work for other businesses. It is your responsibility to make sure they keep your production on track. They can only do that if you are organised and are not given a reason to take their eyes off the ball.

Bad communication - if you cannot communicate what you want, you will not get what you need. Manufacturers are not clairvoyants. They cannot read your mind. Often you will work with people in another country, from another culture, who speak another language to you. Being able to communicate clearly with them and convey your ideas, instructions and expectations is vitally important. How this happens is ON YOU. Not on them. Obviously, they play a part in it, but it is your business and your money ultimately. It is your responsibility to ensure they are clear on what they have to do and how to do it. This means that you need to communicate in every way and method possible until they are crystal clear on what they are expected to do and deliver.

Communication can be in audio format (phone call, voice message), visual (drawing, sketch, tech pack, video call, video file) and written (email, contract, purchase order, spec sheet). If you do not speak the same language, use all available tools and translate for extra clarity. Back up what you are trying to explain with visuals. And finally, always, always, always document and create a paper trail of conversations, agreements made, and deliverables agreed upon. Leave nothing of any importance to chance, and you will have an infinitely easier time.

Lack of trust - as with any human relationship, trust is at the core of everything. Trust is not a given; it is earned. It takes a long time to earn and seconds to lose. Cliche this may be, but it is true nonetheless. Many manufacturers have learned not to trust designers who approach them and make enquiries because of bitter experiences along the way. They have learned not to trust for a reason. That is not to say they can't and won't trust, but you have to earn it. And vice versa.

Not all manufacturers are honest and have the best of intentions. So they too have to earn your trust. It is your duty to do checks in advance of working with them and use your common sense at all times to ensure you are not taken for a ride. You need to take it slowly and build up the trust between you. Talk is cheap, so look beyond words for evidence and vice versa. Do not start a new business relationship by spinning stories of how talented you are, what dreams and hopes you have and how they should help you and trust you and do all you ask...blah blah blah...Be professional and build up trust.

If you understand the above and integrate it into your daily business practice, not only will your manufacturing run smoothly, but I am sure many other areas of your business will benefit too.

Finding The Right Manufacturer...For You And Your Brand

I am sure you can see by now how finding the right manufacturer, without understanding the above, might seem like an impossible task. And rightly so. You weren't born knowing how to stand up, take your first steps and gain confidence to walk and run overnight. Manufacturing (and, in fact, running a fashion business) is just the same. You need to build up the knowledge, skills, and mindset required and improve on it with every manufacturing order you place.

Knowing the above will help you immeasurably to find manufacturers. But finding THE RIGHT one for you requires a little extra knowledge.

I am a great believer that one has to find the right manufacturer for them (as a person) and for the business, they are running. If you are to work well and trust the person you work with, you need to like them and be able to grow to trust them as a result.

Trust comes as a result of liking and getting to know someone.

So finding the right personality fit is important. I am not saying find a new best friend, but find someone you don't dread calling and asking for professional advice, discussing a problem and checking the status of your samples and production.

Specialists vs Generalists

Then, they must be able to do the job. They must be the right fit for your product.

Just because someone has a factory, people and machines inside it and say they can make what you ask for and describe doesn't mean that they can or are right for the job.

Some manufacturers have a scarcity mindset. They are afraid of being left with no work and hence are always overpromising and under-delivering. They say "yes" to everything and anything just to make sure they have cash flowing in. This is wrong but cannot be stopped. Instead, it is your responsibility to ensure you draw up a selection criterion for yourself and vet strictly against it.

There are countless "jack of all trades" types of small manufacturers that are masters of nothing. You want to avoid them like the plague unless your product is a simple, generic run of the mill and you are not bothered about the quality that much.

You want to find the "Masters of one trade" type of manufacturers, a.k.a the specialists. The ones who are very clear on what they are best at, what they do, who they work with, what they charge and how they charge.

As I explained in an earlier chapter, a sewing machine cannot sew every type of fabric equally well. Even the most skilled and best seamstress cannot sew expertly on every type of material. All materials are not made the same, do not behave the same way, cannot be treated and sewn in the same manner.

Most large factories working for mainstream, mass-market brands are used to working with woven or knit fabrics and sewing nothing overly complicated. If your brand is more premium, your designs are more complicated, and your fabrics are expensive and delicate, you want to find factories and skilled machinists who know how to execute your design and handle your materials. This applies not just to garments but also to leatherwoods, jewellery, shoes...and almost everything.

How To Search For Manufacturers?

Above all, you need to be clear on what you are looking for. You need to be clear on what skills and machines you want them to have. You need to ask who else they work for, their past track record of clients, see examples of their work and visit them.

You need to ask them what they specialise in and not be afraid to push to get an answer on this. Factory owners often will be scared of saying something that may cost them a potential new client - but as far as I am concerned, it is important to do all necessary to discover if someone is right or wrong as soon as possible. If they are struggling (aka reluctant) to tell you - ask the opposite - what would they absolutely not touch and work with.

I was once in one such situation, and no matter what I asked, I was told by the friendly factory owner that they were amazing, they can do anything (for me!), work on any design no matter how complex, with any fabric - I should just trust them and give them a chance. They would lower their minimum requirements, help me out,...do all I ask. After I exhausted all possibilities of finding out what they are great at, I reversed my questioning strategy. I asked what product they could NOT do. Again, I was told they could do it all. Then I asked, "what materials will you not work with?" and he said - we will not work with silk.

Boom! Finally! They will NOT work with silk...?! That was huge. If they won't work with silk, it means they will not work with delicate materials. Which meant they could not do special occasions and evening wear, which meant they could not do everything and certainly could not work on high-end garments production. One simple word told me volumes.

I did end up working with this manufacturer and, over time, referring many brands to his factory (as he is brilliant), but I only referred brands looking for daywear clothing production at the mid-market level.

So, in short, do all you can and find out all you can in advance, before you spend time and money sampling with disappointing results. One of the best ways to get all the answers to your questions in a record short time is to visit the manufacturers.

Visiting Factories

I am often asked if one should visit their manufacturer? How important is it to do so, and how often should you do it?

My answer always is the same - YES! You absolutely must visit your manufacturers, it is super important, and you should do it as often as possible. Period.

Visiting your manufacturer allows you to put a face to the name. It allows you to build a relationship. It also means that you get to see, with your own eyes, what words may not be able to communicate. You get to see and meet the people who will work on your products, and making a good impression on them goes a long way too. Being respectful, acknowledging them, bringing a box of chocolates for the workers, striking a conversation if you can, having the opportunity, and being polite and curious are all small gestures that mean a huge amount to these people. They will remember how you made them feel. They will repay you back often by taking better care of your production. You cannot buy this kind of attention.

When you visit factories, you can also get faster and more accurate answers to your questions. Sometimes you don't even have to ask to be able to see and know.

Small things like seeing how they treat their staff or other brands' production will tell you how you will be treated and your production. If you are concerned about copying and protecting your designs and the factory owner swears to not show your products to others but is happy to show you everyone else's, what would you believe? His words or actions. Unless you visit the factory, you will only have the words to hang on to.

If they tell you how they do everything in-house and quality control is paramount to them, but you cannot see the entire production cycle taking place under one roof, what would you believe? What you see or what you hear?

I personally love visiting factories and seeing for myself how they operate and are structured, connecting to the people who work on my products and feeling the overall vibe often tells me all I need to know. Aside from that, the next best thing is that I always, without fail, learn new things about manufacturing that will help me later.

Your manufacturers' knowledge is an untapped resource that can bring you much success if you learn how to use it to your best advantage and interest.

Here is a curious example for you. Years ago, when I was working for a luxury leather goods brand, we often had customers complain that some of our very expensive products made of very natural leather would easily scratched and mark. They always asked what they could do to remove the scratches. I shared what I knew, but one time, while visiting the factory making these products, I stopped and asked the master craftsman - an elderly man who had spent his entire life making leather goods - what he would suggest I advise the customers. He looked up, grabbed a wallet from his machine and scratched it gently with a nail. Then ran his thumb over his sweaty forehead and rubbed the mark left by his nail on the surface of the leather. After a few gentle rubs, the scratch was gone. We laughed a lot, and I walked away that day with a story to tell our customers and an inexpensive solution to a common problem.

So as you can see, visiting factories is a must, and it should be done as often as possible. And if your factory is far and it is not possible to do it often, then do it as often as you can. Rarely is better than never. Plan for it and factor this cost into your development budget. And in-between visits, use available technology to your advantage. Arrange for online face to face meetings, ask them to take you on a tour of the factory via their phone camera and simply think outside the box. Where there is a will, there is a way.

Minimum Order Quantity (MOQ)

Most factories you will encounter tend to quote a minimum order of units they require per design to accept to work with you. Of course, some factories do not have such requirements. As a general rule of thumb, you pay more for manufacturing if there are no minimums or low MOQ. The higher the MOQ, the bigger the factory, the lower the price per unit.

Factories, as I said earlier, are businesses like any other. In order to grow and be sustainable, they must have healthy finances. Ensuring that they get the right kind of work through their doors and that the work they undertake is done efficiently and get paid at the end of it is essential for their business survival and profitability.

Most factories calculate the prices they quote for manufacture based on the time it takes them to make the product. Therefore, most factories can tell you what every minute of time costs and every minute of the machinists' time is accounted for.

So, with this in mind, making sure they work efficiently and that the work they accept will bring in the right amount of money requires them to set a MOQ for their customers. They have to plan their time. They have to work to a tightly planned manufacturing schedule and ensure their workers' time is utilised most efficiently. This cannot happen with small orders, no MOQ and unorganised customers.

On the other hand, MOQs, while necessary, can also act as gatekeepers. They filter the good from the bad enquiries. Often, if you strike a really good relationship with the person you speak to and then enquire about MOQ, you will find that those are not set in stone. There is room for negotiation. So, again, there are no set rules, and it's very personal.

In my *Fashion Manufacturing Mastery* online course, I detail all of the manufacturing topics covered here and more. There is an entire module on MOQ and how to negotiate them, but if you are a small brand looking for manufacturers with low to no MOQ requirements, be warned that this comes at a higher cost.

CMT vs FF

In manufacturing, you have two main methods of working with factories.

CMT stands for Cut, Make, Trim. Smaller factories tend to operate this model. As a client, you must provide them with everything they will need to make your sample or production. They, in turn, will provide the labour and trims (in most cases, this means the thread only).

So, you buy and deliver to the factory patterns, fabrics, linings, hardware and accessories. When they have absolutely everything, they will Cut the materials as per your patterns, they will Make (assemble) the product as per your instructions (and approved sealed sample) and use their Trim (thread) to do so. They will charge you for the time it took them to make the product
(pre-agreed for production), and voila. Job done.

By contrast, larger brands who work with larger factories work on a Fully Factored (FF) basis. They will place the order with the factory and then collect and pay for the finished goods at the agreed time. The price they will pay includes all the materials required and a small surcharge for the organisational duties and risk undertaken by the manufacturer to purchase in advance all of the materials to fulfil the order. Large brands do not get involved in sourcing and buying materials for production. They may do so at the sampling stage but not for production. They literally pass an order and pay for the finished product.

Personally, I am not a great fan of CMT because it ultimately leads to pricing issues and undervaluing the true cost involved in making the product. The loss is entirely for the designer, and sometimes they lose much more than they gain. But I also think that working CMT for small and new brands is often a rite of passage and the only possible option they have at that stage of business.

Working on a CMT basis with factories quickly teaches creative entrepreneurs the intricacies of the manufacturing process and opens the eyes to all the little and large things that can go wrong.

Working on an FF basis with factories as a smaller brand is not impossible. But you need to have a better understanding of the manufacturing industry. There are multiple ways you can do that, and they too are outlined in the Fashion Manufacturing Mastery course.

Local vs Global

Before the pandemic, many brands manufactured locally if they were smaller and less experienced and farther away (near or offshore) if they wanted cheaper production and if they had more confidence navigating the fashion industry. Post pandemic, the manufacturing landscape has changed.

No matter what brand you have or are planning on creating, there is a case for having both local and offshore manufacturing.

Here is how this may look and work.

If you are just starting out, finding a local factory to work with is wise. This way, you get to learn about sampling, as well as manufacturing your range. Working locally means you can visit more often, react faster when necessary, have lower MOQ and have less of a cultural difference and language barriers standing in your way.

On the downside, however, it might mean that you will have to pay a higher cost for something that elsewhere, farther afield may cost you less.

Manufacturing near (another country close to yours) or offshore (another continent, usually this term is used for manufacturing in Asia and the Far East) would mean higher logistics costs, travel costs, less face to face time with your factory, potentially quality problems and misunderstandings due to cultural and language barriers. It often means higher MOQ, but on the other side, production prices often are lower.

In today's day and age, you need both local and offshore.

Local manufacturing allows for a faster turnaround of your orders. If the factories you work with also have low MOQ, it means you can react faster to market trends or launch limited edition collections and test the market before embarking on a bigger commitment financially. Working with local factories also means that should there be (again) circumstances preventing us from travelling freely, your business does not have to suffer. Yes, the costs may be higher in terms of manufacture, but they can be offset by the lower logistics costs, the faster turn around, the greater control you can exercise over the end quality of the products and smarter choices you make in terms of materials and design. All in all, having a factory nearby to work with has plenty of advantages and can be an invaluable business asset.

But, as you grow, you'll need to make bigger production orders and lower your costs, in order to grow your margin and profitability. As you grow and hire more people, you can achieve better systems optimisation and therefore better plan ahead manufacturing. Working with larger factories farther away would be better as you develop core collections of products that you sell all year round. Depending on your location, you may or may not have a larger factories nearby. If the latter is the case, perhaps going offshore is the only way to scale your production.

Learning how to handle manufacturing near and far and deciding what to manufacture where comes with experience. It cannot be rushed, and you should not rush it. But as always, awareness of the possibilities is important. Thinking creatively and strategically will help you grow your brand faster and increase your profitability.

Big successful fashion brands have many factories that they work with. Often they have more than one factory that makes the same product as a form of security and protection in case something happens with one of them. Big brands learn fast that they cannot and should not have all their "eggs in one basket." This working approach is something that gets implemented over time. Yet, it is important to have this awareness from day one of your business and work towards this growth strategy.

You Can't Have It All…Right Now

Almost all start-ups and small brands struggle to find the right manufacturer because they have an impossible wish list. They want a factory that will be:

- Local (because they are a "sustainable" brand).

- Low or no MOQ (because they are just starting out and have no financial resources and are scared to commit).

- Not charge too much (they want to make their money last longer and sell cheaper but still make a profit).

- Able to produce a high quality finished product (they know customers are educated and fussy).

- Certified (bonus ask for a few of the more "knowledgeable" creatives out there. They can use this as a marketing badge of honour).

All of the above are impossible to achieve as a small brand, and some are mutually exclusive. Or let me rephrase, you can have any two or 3 at most, at one time but not all.

I will quickly explain why this is an impossible wish list, but again, in my *Fashion Manufacturing Mastery* course, I go much more in-depth, and you can access the course here: https://www.fashioninsiderstraining.com/fmm

Local manufacturing (particularly if by "local" we refer to a western country location) means that there will be a minimum wage requirement in place. Therefore nothing you make will be "cheap."

Low MOQ or even no MOQ means that you will pay more per unit, as explained earlier.

High-quality manufacturing comes with having highly skilled machinists work on your products and not rush the make of your production. Therefore that will come at a higher price.

And last but not least, factory auditing and certifications are very costly and only large factories can afford to have them. This means that smaller factories will not have them, and if they do, they will charge more and require MOQ to work with.

So, the trick here is to know what you need, what is most important to you as a brand and compromise. Out of the above 5 points, one or two at most will be more important to your business than the rest. Focus on what makes sense to your brand and will help you run and grow, and is valuable to your customers. The rest you can "park" for later when your business is bigger and requires a different set of priorities.

The Three Sins Of Manufacturing

Over the many years I have worked in the fashion industry, manufactured products for small and large brands and mentored countless brand creative founders and teams, I have boiled down the colossal manufacturing mistakes repeatedly made to the following three "sins" (as I call them):

Need: When you are in a tight spot, in a great need and in a rush to find a manufacturer fast because someone let you down and you need to meet deadlines; your factory burnt down, or it messed up badly, and you can't trust them to fix it, or you had a falling out with the factory owner, whatever the reason when you are in a state of "need," you will make rushed, emotional decisions and almost always they will lead to problems.

My advice is to take your time. Cancel orders if you have to, but make a choice and a decision to work with someone only when you have checked them out. You are as certain as you can be that they are right for you and your product.

Greed: Anytime you choose based on a lower, better price, you will pay for it through the nose later. Just as you cannot compete on price with your competitors, you also cannot pick a manufacturer based on a lower price quote. Accepting a lower price could mean any and all of the following: people are not paid properly, quality will not be as you want it, corners will be cut, they will be overpromising and under-delivering, you will be paying the difference in another way, they may be using you as a gap filler, and nothing will run on time.

Basically, more often than not, these situations spell problems to come. Don't be greedy.

Vanity: Because the fashion industry feeds on ego and operates on a "smoke and mirror" model, being seen to be in the right circles means a lot to many creatives. Manufacturing in the same factory as (insert your favourite, famous, globally recognised brand here) surely adds gravitas and weight to your own brand and makes it instantly more successful in the eyes of others.

No! This couldn't be further from the truth. In fact, big brands manufacture with big factories. Big factories rarely accept to work with small brands for many reasons, but the most common one would be that small brands cannot meet big factories' MOQ requirements.

So, using your common sense, try to think of a good reason why a big factory that works with big well-known brand clients will agree to work with a small unknown and unproven, most likely financially strained brand?

Doesn't the above make you wonder what's in it for them? Oh, and by the way, if they just tell you these famous brands are their customers, don't believe everything you hear. Ask for proof and recommendations and see how they respond.

The fact is, acting out of vanity comes at a very high price, so beware and be warned. Use your common sense, forget about your ego and make the right business decision.

Ethical Manufacturing

Over the years, the human population has evolved and become more sensitive to human rights. Global environmental issues and social movements have greatly affected how we think and see human life. Of course, this has affected the requirements creative entrepreneurs place on their businesses and their expectations from the people they work with.

Often in manufacturing, there is talk about fair pay, child labour, human rights, etc. While I am all for it, I want to put forward another point of view that is not really much spoken about.

Most western creative entrepreneurs and fashion designers, despite insisting to work with manufacturers that are ethical and pay fairly their employees, proceed to haggle and negotiate lower prices once they meet a factory that they feel is good enough for them to work with. They think it is acceptable to squeeze the manufacturer and not pay them in full for the smallest of reasons. I even know of instances where designers and big brand financial controllers have a rule never to pay an invoice in full (even if agreed).

When you work with factories based in another western country, the laws often protect the workers. There is a minimum wage most workers get paid, and if they are out of work, they get paid unemployment benefits. In counties outside of the West, factory workers located in Asia and other third-world countries do not have the luxuries we take for granted or the legal systems to protect them. The poverty people experience in these countries is something we would never know or comprehend. To expect the level of employer/employee relations that we know of, fair pay, human rights and basic working conditions that we are accustomed to is unreasonable. We have to accept that different cultures and countries have their own rules by which they operate. The people who live there and work in these factories have basic needs and problems we rarely understand.

So, being sensitive to the culture and people you choose to work with is important. Visiting the factories and seeing first hand who you work with and who works and makes your products is important. Recognising these people and giving them the credit due is important. Paying them fairly (and not trying to squeeze them at every chance you may have) and, in fact, finding ways to support and reward them for a job well done is the ethical way to work. Yet no one thinks this way, no one wants to see the reality, and hardly any brands do the right thing.

Whatever criteria you choose to impose and how you judge the factories you select to work with, you should do it within the context of the culture and country this factory operates in, not your own culture and country. See it through the eyes of the people there and be ethical in your dealings with them too. If you advocate for change and better conditions, find the factories that already work as per your standards and offer better conditions to their workers. Support them by choosing to work with them, even if they ask for a bit more than others (and guess why they do that?).

If you plan to develop a long term relationship with the factories of your choice, visit them and invest in their people and community. Be the one to instigate a change in the fashion industry and be part of a change for the better of the industry. The right customers will reward you for it.

Remember one of the ten commandments - what goes around comes around. It applies to the good and the bad!

Terms & Conditions

By now, you would have understood that manufacturing is a complex business.

It's a bit like lego. To make anything, you need to stack many pieces together, and they all have to fit in the right place. To get the right results, you need everyone to play nicely and play by the "rules."

But what are the rules, you might ask? Great question!

In fashion, there are no rules, at least not written ones, because it is convenient not to write them. But this is beginning to change.

Until recently, most suppliers, manufacturers and designers operated on "trust" and some outdated rules written on the back of an order form that no one ever read. Manufacturers would run a mile at the mention of the word "contract." Designers will go round in circles asking others if they use contracts, who has a template to share, only to end up not using it anyway.

These days the industry is changing. Perhaps as a younger generation of savvy, educated factory owners come to run factories, or maybe due to communication moving to be more online, all involved are having to become more "professional." Or maybe it is less scary to mention or request things in writing than in person. Regardless, it is much-needed progress. It is not perfect, some factories still run a mile at the mention of the idea, but this is less and less now. In fact, many factories, even smaller ones, have their own contracts now.

Contracts

The reason so many factory owners are not crazy about the idea of "contracts" is because, in the past, many factories were run by ex-factory workers who lacked higher education. They weren't confident nor affluent enough to retain the services of legal advisors. Contracts they may have signed had ended up badly for them, or they might have heard the countless horror stories going around the industry.

But this is changing. Many factory owners are now younger and well educated. Some have grown up in manufacturing families. Others are Google university graduates. Either way, these days, most people tend to "know" what their "rights" are.

In a process that is as complex as manufacturing and one that involves so many moving parts and so much human error, it is important to have rules and be clear on what they are, who is responsible for what and what happens if.

That is all a "contract" is and should be, in my opinion. In fact, I often encourage brands I work with to reframe it and see it as a "working agreement." Instead of going to a lawyer and paying a huge amount of money for a piece of paper no one understands or paying for a template from the internet, I believe it is better to draft your own or ask your manufacturer if they have one and use it as a starting point.

Read through it and adapt it to reflect the working relationship between the two parties - you and the manufacturer. (To be clear, I am not saying don't seek legal advice. Of course, do so by all means, but make sure the legal professional understands the fashion industry and drafts a fair and reasonable contract reflecting the reality of the industry.)

Working agreements cannot be one-sided. I have seen in the past so-called contracts that were all on the side of the designer. They contained a list of veiled threats such as, if you make a mistake, you pay for it; if you are late with the delivery, we will deduct X per cent off the total etc. No wonder factories ghosted designers.

Contracts are only effective if they are understood and respected by both parties. There has to be a clear outline of both party responsibilities, timelines and what happens if they are missed. Clear agreement on payment terms, what happens in the event of payment or production delay, what happens if either party cancels, unforeseen disasters etc.

Both parties must agree and be happy to sign it. Treating it as an important part of the process that is there to protect both parties and speak openly about it. Being open to discussing and amending it until everyone is happy is the best way to get one signed by your manufacturer.

Non Disclosure Agreements (NDA)

Since everything nowadays ends up on the internet, design ideas and products are easily stolen and copied. Proving how it happened isharder.

Many designers worry about the manufacturer leaking their designs to others or copying them themselves. It is true. This does happen sometimes. It is not that common, but it happens. What can you do to protect yourself?

One popular belief is that having a Non Disclosure Agreement (NDA) in place will protect you. This is not quite accurate, however. In most cases, the NDAs designers give to factories to sign are not worth the paper they are written on. Often they are templates downloaded from the internet that are too generic and unspecific to be of any value.

Also, proving how your design idea was leaked and your product copied is also hard to prove.

But should you wish to have your factory sign an NDA make sure your document has the following important components that can be helpful, in case you need it:

- Specific – what exactly is the design idea or element that is truly yours and already does not exist on the market you want to protect. You cannot protect and claim as yours something that already exists and is in use. A dress in itself is not unique. But a particular construction detail or design feature can be.

- Time-bound – you cannot ban someone from forever and ever not doing something. You cannot accuse someone of leaking your design ideas when everyone these days feeds off the same inspiration sources. Even legally registered patents are only protected for 10 years or so. Be clear and state for how long this NDA is valid for.

Get someone with a legal background and experience in copyright protection to advise you on the best way to protect your Intellectual Properties and creative assets.

A word of caution. NDAs may look like useful protection to have, but I beg to disagree. They are hard to enforce and even harder to prove. In my opinion, they act more as a deterrent. A signal that you are serious and mean business. Also, factories work with so many clients and see so many designs. How would you know if they have or have not seen something just like your design idea in the past? Or a version of it? What makes you so certain your idea is so unique and new?

Last but not least, in fashion, one only needs to change a few small design elements for a design to no longer be considered the same as another. In a fashion system with no clear rules about protection and no consequences to fear, "copying" is almost an intrinsic part of the industry. Often disputes are settled behind closed doors only out of fear of reputational damage (which is harder to recover from), not because there is an admission of wrongdoing.

By all means, have one if you wish to, but do not rely on it solely for protection.

Payment Terms & Financing (invoice factoring)

Again, there is nothing set in stone as far as payment terms are concerned. There are no actual rules, except the rules people make for themselves and believe are the rules. Whoever has the upper hand makes the rules.

One of the biggest sources of pain, stress and loss of money comes because of factories making unreasonable demands. Fearful and desperate creatives forget to use common sense and agree to follow "the rules."

So let's bust this myth and hopefully save your sanity and money.

When it comes to manufacturing, the most quoted payment terms are 50/50. In other words, 50% of the total value of the order, paid at the time of placing the order. (Many manufacturers will not accept or put the order in their system until payment has been received.)

The second 50% is payable before delivery. So in effect, the manufacturer gets paid upfront before you get your goods.

On many occasions, some small factories dealing with small startups that are completely new to the fashion industry (and therefore clueless) will be told they have to pay 100% on placing orders. And many do!

Let's make an analogy. Imagine needing a doctor for a surgery and finding one on the internet or being referred to one. You speak to them; they say they can treat you and even operate on you. They assure you this is what they do. You ask questions, and everything seems to check out. They tell you who they have operated on in the past. You don't know these people, and even if you know of them, you don't ask them for reference. You just believe what you are told. Then you are asked to pay for everything upfront, in advance, before the surgery, and you do so, trusting that they will do as they promised. Will you be happy to be operated on?

Imagine there are no google ratings to refer to, no "trip advisor" style reviews to read and rely on. All you can do is trust and hope for the best. Would you pay everything in advance? I really hope your answer is an immediate and confident HELL NO! (If you took your time to think about it and weigh the pros and cons, and if anything less than a resounding HELL NO was your answer, I'd be worried if I were you.)

And yet, many do just that. Pay in advance to strangers large amounts of money without having enough evidence that they will do what they promise. Then they cry when they do not see any results or get far, far, worse than they expected.

If you take away just one thing from this chapter, then let it be this: **do not part with your money until you are certain you are getting what you are paying for.**

What can you do instead?

Negotiate!

50/50 is indeed a widely used payment term. Especially as you work for the first time with someone. But as time goes on and you both get to know each other and trust between you grows. It is up to you and in your interest as the steward of your brand and business to steer the working relationship to better payment terms.

The logic of the 50/50 is the following. 50% paid on order placement is a form of deposit for the manufacturer. In case you cancel, they have not totally wasted their time for nothing. It also helps with their cash flow since many factories pay wages weekly and not monthly.

The other 50% requested to be paid before delivery protects the manufacturer from complaints and disputes that often arise once production is delivered. It means they wash their hands off of the faults and any remedial work they agree to do becomes subject to new chargeable agreements. Not to mention again that it helps cashflow.

If you are a small brand and entering into a new relationship with a factory, you will struggle to negotiate better payment terms, to begin with. But here is what you can do:

• Put milestones and checkpoints along the way to ensure you will get what you pay for.

• Regularly check on manufacturing progress and ask for photos. Visit if you can and check on the progress of your production order and that all is as you want it to be. Having a sealed sample and a clear documented tech pack to follow is not only a good practice but essential.

• Give clear instructions on what the acceptable quality for your product looks like. In the *Fashion Manufacturing Mastery* course, there is a whole module on quality control and how to create a process that works for you and will protect you from mistakes.

• Before the final payment, make sure you check the quality of all products. Either go in person or send someone trusted, who knows your products, to check your production and ensure it is all correct. Once you make this last payment, it is super hard to then have corrections made. But if you haven't paid, it's in the factories interest to fix anything you are not happy with to get paid.

• If you cannot visit in person or send someone, arrange for a few randomly selected pieces from your production to be sent to you to check and approve prior to payment. You can ask anything you spot at this point (in writing with visual documentation) to be fixed across the entire production.

• Negotiate better payment terms - 40/60, 30/70, 30/30/40 (on order, at certain checkpoints during production and pre-shipment). It is your duty to try, and all they can say is NO. But usually, if you are reasonable and have developed a good relationship up until that point with your manufacturer, then they will be willing to work out a new agreement, something that works for you both. If they don't, consider the possibility that they will be even more unreasonable and difficult to deal with if and when problems arise.

Critical Path

One of the biggest complaints factories make towards fashion brands is their lack of sense of urgency. Creatives often do not have a clear timeline to work to and expect things to happen yesterday.

It is an everyday occurrence for brands, especially start-ups, to contact a factory for the first time and say that they need production next week or next month. Is it any wonder that they never hear back from a factory after such an enquiry?

On average, almost all factories will quote for production 6 -12 weeks - depending on how they work. Any promises for less will usually result in delays. If I were you, I would also add some buffer and allow more time, on top of what they quote, as delays always occur somewhere along the way.

So with that in mind, the onus, as ever, is on you, the creative brand owner, to make a realistic plan, a realistic timeline and allow plenty of time for things to be done.

If you know when you want to launch a new collection, work backwards and take into account the following:

• How long in advance do you need your samples for photography?
• How long the factory needs to complete a production order?
• How long does it take for materials to be made and shipped?
• How long does it take for you to sample?
• How long does it take for you to finalise your patterns?
• How long would it take you to design and refine your design?

...and anything else you can think of.

Add to all the above buffers at every step of the way, and you will get to a date when you can consider the start of your creative process. Or you can work out a date in the future that can be a realistic date for the launch of something new.

Working to a critical path is an important part of manufacturing. Having a critical path to work will save you a lot of time and money and often your reputation.

All in all, the manufacturing process, as you would have seen by now, is one of the key business stages all brands must master.

Without a good reliable source of manufacture, you have no business.

Without good organisation, trust, and good communication, you will have bigger problems than you could cope with.

Getting to grips with the mindset, knowledge and systems required to get the end products you want, pay for, and will be bought by your customers is key.

Some creatives are simply not wired in the necessary way to be able to procure their own production. Realise this and get help if this sounds like you. Do not hope and pray it will somehow work out. It won't. Others are good at it but may not want to do it, as it is a very time consuming and draining process. Again, get help. Set up better systems and checkpoints to ensure you don't run into trouble. Pay extra if you must to get what you need.

And above all, use your common sense. Take your time. Question things. Listen to your gut. If something doesn't feel right, stop and double-check. Manufacturing is a business like any other. People must make money and so must you!

6

Pricing For Profit

Price is what you pay, value is what you get.

Warren Buffett

When I was growing up, I was terrible at math. Terrible! I used to sit in the back row with my school friends and read books. We devoured classic novels, mostly during math lessons. Over the years, I believed the story I had made up in my head that I was bad with numbers. I had such a fear of numbers that once, after detailed calculations of how much some shared expenses between a friend and I had to be split, I concluded and for a while believed that what I owed was owed to me simply because I was "scared" to go over the numbers again.

When I worked for large brands, merchandising meetings were painful as everyone spoke in numbers and percentages. It felt like they were taking another language at times. Until one day, I sat with a friend who helped me make sense of the numbers and what I believed were complicated formulas. I created an easier way to process the main calculations used in the industry and get to the same results as everyone else. A much more basic and simple way, but just as effective, and I was free to get involved in these meetings and "fight" over product cancellations and margins.

I share these stories because I think many creatives are just like me. They have created stories, they believe, around numbers and avoid anything math-related. The reality is, we are not bad at numbers at all. We just missed registering some of the basics at school, perhaps, then continued to struggle with math and ended up believing that we are terrible with numbers. This leads to shying away from looking at the numbers in our fashion business, which, in turn, my friends, is a recipe for disaster.

Let me show you how you can begin to take your power back.

The Art of Pricing

Most young brand owners I speak to have no idea what their profit margin is.

Almost all creatives I speak to, who ask me for advice about going into wholesale, have no idea their existing pricing structure is not set up for wholesale.

Most fashion entrepreneurs busy creatively have no idea what "break-even" means, let alone what it would take to get to the break-even point in their business.

I don't blame them either. It is not easy to find the information presented in an easy to digest way, especially in the context of fashion.

Let's make it super simple for you to understand the basics and apply them in the future. Because if you want your fashion brand to succeed and grow, you need to know your numbers and talk numbers freely and with confidence.

Pricing Models

If you go into the fashion business as a product brand (and not offering services), you have two main ways of pricing your products.

Direct To Consumer Sales Model, a.k.a. DTC (D2C)

The internet has made it possible for anyone to operate a business by themselves and sell directly to the consumer, owning all the data and being in full control along the way.

The downside: it's harder to grow your authority. Not impossible, though, just harder.

On the flip side, the positives are many.

By selling DTC, you are able, as a brand, to retain full control of the customer journey, the data you gather along the way and keep the entire profit margin to yourself as a business.

You can immediately be a global player in the global fashion retail industry by selling DTC, which is mainly performed online.

Usually, DTC brands price up their products between 2-4 times the full cost price of the product. In other words, if your final product cost is $100, you will sell your product on the market anywhere between $200-$400, perhaps even more. How you choose to price your product depends on your market penetration strategy.

The lower the price, the more you need to sell to make money - i.e. break-even or profit.

The higher the multiple you use, the faster you'll get to breaking even, and the better the gross profit margin will be.

You do not have to stick to one multiple, as you will see why further below. You can price products some higher, some lower. The main thing to know here is your average gross profit margin and which products have higher margins, so you push them more.

You can sell DTC via your own eCommerce website, but it can also take the form of a bricks-and-mortar shop of your own, a pop-up or taking concession space in another store. Each option comes with different associated costs, so you must research it properly before jumping into it. But, the more routes to market you participate in, the more you'll sell, and the visibility for your brand will increase faster.

Whatever your choice, direct to consumer is the future of retail. Until recently (before the internet), there was almost no choice.

Wholesale Sales Model, a.k.a WS

Prior to the onset of the internet, the only way to sell directly to the consumer was by opening a stand-alone shop. This, for obvious reasons, wasn't such an easily available option to many. So all they were then left with was to wholesale their product.

Wholesale meant that they would sell their products, at a certain price, to a buyer from a small boutique or a larger retailer, who in turn would add their markup and sell on to their target customers. To reach these buyers, brands had to pay to participate in trade fairs, pay agencies to represent them and pay PR companies to generate press for them in order to become more attractive to the buyers. When I was getting started with my jewellery brand, I wrote to the buyer of my favourite department store at the time. She was kind enough to spare five minutes and see me and my small collection. She liked it but told me she wouldn't buy anything at this time. She told me that without any press coverage or other stockists, my brand was a "hard buy."

To make money, brands had to sell in volume. In the process, they didn't gain much in terms of customer data, nor had any stronghold over their customers and brand perception.

Wholesale is no longer the only way for brands to sell their products. Luckily, DTC brings in many more opportunities and possibilities. And yet, wholesale has a firm place and advantages for brands who understand how the fashion industry works and create well-thought-through strategic business plans.

Let me explain. Securing a few good, authoritative wholesale accounts is a key tactic if a brand wants to build authority fast. While a brand may not make much money this way unless they sell a lot of products through this channel, being stocked by reputable retailers next to aspirational competitor brands can have a magical effect. Suddenly, the brand could get noticed overnight and gain a higher status in a way that press and marketing cannot deliver on.

To be able to wholesale, your product must be priced at least 5-6 times the product cost price. This is because you, as a brand, must keep some margin as well as the retailer who will sell the product on.

Here is how the math works:

If your total product cost comes to $100, your product will need to sell on the market for at least $500-$600.

Here is how this is calculated:

(Product cost) $100 x 2 = $200. This is your wholesale price. The price that you will quote to wholesale buyers wishing to purchase your products.

When they buy your product, retail buyers will mark up the product they bought anywhere between x2 to x3 or maybe even more. The mark up depends on the product category and on the type of retailer they are buying for.

Slower moving goods like fine jewellery, for example, will have a lower mark up, i.e. they usually get marked up x2 from cost to recommended retail price (RRP).

Faster moving goods get marked up by a higher multiple.

Most fashion boutiques selling clothes and accessories mark up their goods around x2.7/2.85 times the wholesale price. Larger retailers like big department stores, who have higher expenses and invest more in advertising, may multiply the wholesale price by 3 and more to get to an RRP that works for them. Why? Because they have higher operating costs and invest in advertising and marketing more than smaller retailers.

In order to wholesale your collections, you need to plan your collections in such a way as to attract buyers. Also, your brand must have sufficient financial funds to be able to put into manufacturing a larger volume of production.

Naturally, not all will be paid by your business upfront, but still, the risk for your business is bigger.

Hybrid Sales Model a.k.a DTC + WS

However, in recent years and particularly since the pandemic, it has become more important than ever for brands to have direct access to their customers.

Even the luxury brands who dragged their feet into eCommerce and were almost the last to develop commercial shoppable portals got there in the end.

Owning your route to market is definitely the best way forward. It allows the brand to collect valuable data based on tweaking, improving, and developing the business further.

But, doing it alone is infinitely harder. It requires stronger marketing skills, and no brand can scale in any meaningful way and fast enough by simply relying on word of mouth and organic traffic. Paid advertising will most definitely be required.

And even then, there is the challenge of creating desirability and authority for the brand. Not an easy task to do out of context and alone.

That is where wholesale plays such a nice role and plugs the holes the direct to consumer model appears to have.

Being seen in the right place, next to the right brands, adds instant credit in next to no time - so long as you manage to get to that position.

Adding wholesale to your brand development strategy allows for faster and more credible brand positioning.

This strategic move, in my opinion, in today's day and age, is not so much about making a profit but creating leverage to use in your DTC operations.

So, here is how the hybrid model can be deployed.

Ambitious smaller and growing brands must be strategic about how they grow their sales alongside their authority and visibility. Finding a happy medium between DTC and wholesale is a key part of a successful sales and marketing strategy.

Wholesale can be profitable in time, but to begin with, one must see it as a brand positioning exercise. It pays off by the extra opportunities it brings and the new doors it opens.

If you do decide to operate a hybrid sales model, you must aim for 4-6 plus times multiple of your cost price.

In other words, by pricing your product x4 of cost price, you will be able to just about selectively sell to some wholesalers but not make any profit. Your goal would be to break even.

If you are able to price your goods at a higher multiple - x5 or x6 - you will be able to make a small profit margin and allow a nice margin to your buyer.

If you want to wholesale but cannot price your products any higher than x4, be selective about who you sell to. Over time, as you build your business and your sales increase, you can buy more materials, place bigger production orders (maybe even move to a different manufacturer) and marginally improve on your product costs and expand your profit margin.

Also, it is good practice to increase your prices by a little annually to account for inflation and increased materials and labour costs. By doing so, you also have a chance to increase your margin from the operational side of things too.

Most brands on the market operate at a margin they are not happy with and are always looking to improve. So if you feel like you aren't where you want to be, take comfort in knowing you are not alone.

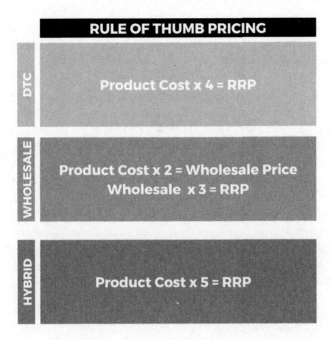

Online Marketplaces

Joining online marketplaces is similar to wholesale, except you own the stock until sold. The risk of it is entirely yours.

Similar to wholesale, marketplaces have a place in the sales strategy but cannot be THE strategy and single route to market. Just as in wholesale, selling via marketplaces means you do not have direct access to your potential customers and have little or no control over how your brand is treated and portrayed.

There is no harm in joining some of them, especially if they have a good reputation and attract sufficient traffic to their website, and the traffic converts to sales. Joining marketplaces often costs you nothing like a brand but your time and the responsibility to ensure you have the stock inventory listed. Sales often are slow to come, and in many cases, it takes months to even get one sale. Marketplaces more often than not operate on a drop shipping basis and tend to charge anything from 15 – 35+ per cent of the RRP price.

So while many do not charge a joining fee, do not forget that your time is your asset, and that comes at a cost to your business. How and where you spend your time and effort directly correlates to the results you'll get for your business.

Unless the marketplace you join is large scale marketplaces like Amazon, Etsy, NOTHS and the like. These giant eCommerce businesses offer many more opportunities for brands to generate sales. If this is the right market channel for you, joining this type of marketplace can be a smart move as you can sell your products, as well as test and validate new product ideas, gather customer reviews and help your overall brand positioning and SEO just by being part of those portals.

But again, I want to emphasise that joining a marketplace is part of a strategically crafted plan but not the way to build your brand. Joining a marketplace can be a distraction since often, these marketplaces rely on the brands they stock to generate marketing for them. By promoting their listing on the marketplace, brands fail to realise that they are actually promoting, for free, someone else's business rather than their own.

So before you commit to one, ask yourself this:

- What's in it for your brand?
- What tangible results can you get, and at what cost?
- Who will bear that cost?

Choosing The Right Model

Knowing what the right balance to strike is, is very individual for every brand.

As a rule of thumb, but by no means a rule to stick to, you can plan for your sales to come 70% from DTC and 30% wholesale. It could be more; it could be less. You may not want to wholesale at all, or you may decide only to offer wholesale sales and not bother with eCommerce (though this is a rather crazy strategy, especially in today's day and age).

Knowing your profit margin, to a large extent, will inform your choices.

If you cannot have a generous margin, you may be more selective with your wholesale accounts and aim to build brand authority at the expense of profits.

If you did have (margin) room to build a more robust wholesale strategy, you may want to work out a stronger and more rounded retail strategy that includes online, offline, full-price, discounted outlets and whatever else takes your fancy.

Whatever you decide on has to reflect your brand's business stage, and it can evolve over time. The main thing is to give enough time to whatever you decide to do, so you can see results and act on that data. You do not have to do everything at the same time. Also, don't decide on doing one thing today and change to another tomorrow because you heard something worked for another brand or someone told you it's better.

Look at the data in front of you and use your common sense, knowledge in your business and yourself and gut feel to make the right choice for you and your business.

Pricing With Profit In Mind

Pricing your products is akin to an art form. It is not a simple equation or formula you can follow. If you do that, you will miss out on "leaving money on the table," as some people refer to underselling products and services.

Pricing also is not something you can do by committee. Asking friends and family what something should cost is the worst possible thing you can do for your business. What something is worth is often a reflection of the self-worth of those giving their opinion. Just don't do it! Your friends and family are (more often than not) not your ideal customers. Most people like bargains, so they would always prefer to get something for a better price.

As a brand founder, only you know what materials and effort have gone into making your product, what the market can bear, and what competitors price similar products.

Basically, never design anything, be it a product or a price, by committee. Ask different questions and get feedback and intel to help you grow your business and sell more, not lose money and get frustrated.

Pricing Basics

When it comes to pricing your product, it is key to keep in mind, always know and be aware of, the following key numbers:

1. Your total product cost price, or Cost of Goods.
2. Your profit margin.
3. Your retail price (i.e. recommended retail price/RRP).

What Is Your Cost of Goods (CoGs)

Your product cost price, referred to in accounting terms as Cost of Goods (or CoGs for short), is an important number to know.

You must always know what it costs you to make your product. If you get this calculation wrong, all your other calculations will be wrong too.

You need to know this number to make sure that you make money when you sell products. After all, making money and making a profit in the process is the goal here. The profits you make will pay your salary and those of your employees and pay for you to run and grow the business. So you do not want to get this number wrong and later wonder why you are always short of money.

Also, if you get this number wrong, you will pay for it by losing profit margin until you find the mistake. Bear in mind that once you announce your pricing to the market, it is really hard to suddenly change it because you found a mistake in your calculations. The sudden jump will be noticed and cast a shadow on your authenticity and honesty as a brand. Trust me. You do not want to damage your reputation that way.

So, how do you get to your total cost price?

Your total product cost comprises the sum of the following parts: raw material and trims, cost of labour, packaging, logistics (i.e. delivery of the product to you), and business admin charge.

MATERIALS + LABOUR + PACKAGING + LOGISTICS + ADMIN FEE = COST OF GOODS

As you sample your product, it is important to keep a list of all the materials that go into making your product, from the smallest to the largest. You can verify this list with your maker to make sure nothing is missed. Whoever works on the sampling and production would be the best person to check and ensure nothing is forgotten.

Years back, I worked for a brand that thought they had a healthy profit margin. When I looked into the Bill of Materials (BoM) to understand the true CoGs, I found plenty of mistakes. Products were missing key material quantities, outdated logistics costs, missing trims and lots more. There was a total disconnect between those who oversaw the sampling and manufacture and those who crunched the numbers. You do not want this to happen to your business.

So include everything and anything used for making the product. If you buy components in bulk, work out the price per unit and add in it. If you are not sure about the usage of materials per product, ask your maker. While you are at it, ask them what the wastage on the materials is and make sure that it is also added to the cost. For example, not every part of the animal hide can be used when you work with leather. It is not unusual to have 20% of waste in every skin. So make sure that the waste is included in the cost, as someone has to pay for it and you don't want it to come out of your profits.

Don't forget to include composition labels, size and branded labels, price tags, care cards, marketing materials you might add with every purchase and basically all the small non-design components that you buy in bulk and add to every product. Many forget that these little items, too, are part of the finished sellable product.

The labour costs will be quoted to you by your maker, including their billable units of time and their own small margin.

If you are a designer-maker responsible for the making of your own products, you must make sure you cost your time properly and charge for your time reasonably and fairly. Most designer-makers cut corners and unknowingly undercharge. Get advice on how to work out your billable hourly rate and keep a tab on how long you take to make one or more products and charge accordingly. If you are too expensive, consider this a sign you should get help and perhaps not be the one running the business and also making the products.

If you work on a Fully Factored basis with a factory, then this part of the costing is easy as they will bill you for the materials, some trims (but not marketing additional materials) and labour in one total cost.

Usually, factories will include some basic packaging in the cost, but check as this may vary from factory to factory. But when it comes to packaging the product received by the end customer, you must take care and add that cost to the cost of the product.

Often designers get carried away with wanting the most beautiful or innovative, different and sustainable packaging, not realising that this cost adds a huge amount to the end product. So keep an eye on this.

Logistics is the cost of transport of the production from the maker to yourself or your storage facility. Most factories work on an **ex-factory** basis. In other words, you, the brand, is responsible for organising and paying for the shipping costs and any tax and duties that may be levied as part of the service.

Investigating the best way to ship your products, by air, road, or sea, will affect your product's end price. So again, take care with this cost. When you know what that cost is, calculate the cost per unit. Over time, as you grow your brand and ship products a few times back and forth, try to work out an approximate percentage that you can work out as a formula. For example, when I worked with leather goods brand manufacturing in Europe and shipping within Europe, I'd worked out, together with the factories I worked with, that shipping small leather goods meant that I could add 3% calculation of the making cost (materials + labour) as shipping. For large leather goods like handbags, this went up to 6%, and so on. The more you can create a rule of thumb and a formula (based on facts and regularly double checked for accuracy), the faster and easier it will be to work out your cost of goods.

Finally, you must always include a small admin charge in the final cost of your goods that will contribute towards the running cost of your business. This can be in the region of 5-10% of CoGs. This small surcharge will contribute to the operational running of your business. In other words, the money will go towards rent, electricity, internet and other core business costs.

The total sum of these parts gives you your Cost of Goods. The final number you come to is the number which, if you use it as a sales price, you won't make nor lose money. It is your **break-even** cost. Any product sold at a sale price below this number will lose you money. You'll be in effect paying from your pocket for people to buy your product. Anything above that number goes towards your gross profit margin.

Calculating Your Profit Margin

Once you have your CoGs number, you can work out your margin.

Here is how:

A. Find out your COGS (cost of goods sold). For example, $100.

B. Find out your revenue/RRP (how much do you sell these goods for, for example, $500).

C. Calculate the gross profit by subtracting the cost from the revenue. $500 – $100 = $400

D. Divide gross profit by revenue: $400 / $500 = 0.8

E. Express it as percentages: 0.8 x 100 = 80%

Or the above expressed as a formula looks like this:

(B – A = C) / B = E x 100 = E%

When you sell your products DTC, you should aim for a 60-75% gross profit margin. Which is the equivalent of pricing your product at a multiple of x 2.5-4. The higher, the better for your business.

If you are selling to retail buyers, you want to aim at a 50% gross profit margin. In other words, you need to double your total product cost (CoGs) and set the wholesale price around that number. It can be a bit higher, can be a little lower, again, it's your decision, but just know the numbers and be aware which products have a better margin and which have lower.

If you operate a hybrid sales model, you need to aim at an 80-85% gross profit margin. This would include a good target wholesale cost margin and a more than healthy margin when selling DTC yourself or selling via a marketplace.

Perception Is Reality

Now here is the bit that people refer to as "art."

Just because 2+2=4 doesn't mean that you should settle on 4 as the final number when it comes to fashion retail.

Sometimes you get simple products that look amazing and are way more expensive than they cost to make. Should you sell them for what it cost you to make them, as per your pricing formula? Or should you arrive at a price that reflects the perceived value of the product?

Other times you might get products that took so much effort to make, the design is great, the materials top grade, and yet, when you do the math, the product simply does not look like it is worth that much. Should you price it the real cost you arrived at by calculating all costs and risk it not selling, just because the formula says so?

The answer to both questions is: it depends!

When you're pricing your products, you need to be aware of your market and how your competitors price similar products. What is your target, ideal customer prepared to pay, given the competition there already is for similar products?

You need to be clear on how your product is better or different from what's already available on the market. You need to factor in intangible factors that add value, like where you manufacture or the authority and reputation you might have created for your brand. Then you price accordingly.

It may be that you have to cut back on your margin and sell it at a lower price. At least you get to make this decision knowingly, right?

It might be that there is an opportunity to price higher and make a much larger margin. Great! Why not if you can, and the product can carry the price.

And sometimes, no matter what you do, it just makes no sense to keep trying to make something work, and you need to "kill your darling."

Many years ago, there was a documentary about Marc Jacobs documenting his time as a creative director for Louis Vuitton. I will never forget one scene when he was sitting around a table with his design team, and they were reviewing some samples for a new collection. They showed a scene where someone from the team pulled a large oversized sweater, which they exclaimed was so ugly. They all wondered what happened for it to turn out so ugly and that there was no way it would sell. Someone had the idea that they should price it ridiculously high as a "one of a kind." I believe the price of two or three thousand dollars was discussed. I don't remember what happened to that sweater, but I remember the shock of realising that you do not have to follow a formula and can "play" with the prices. And, when you are a well-known and desired brand, you can pretty much sell anything as a "one of a kind."

When I was growing my fine jewellery brand, one of my favourite things became pricing new products. I loved the delicate dance between working out the formula and then researching the market for comparative product prices, then looking at my jewellery and assessing if it looked more or less than the price calculated. Was it better and different from my competitors and therefore justified a higher price or not. How did this piece priced at various price points fit into the existing collections? How does it sit within the range it is part of? What does the price say about my brand is it on point or lowering the tone and my brand positioning?

It may sound like hard work, but this part of brand building and growing is essential to your business success and can be very enjoyable.

Under-pricing your products is not a position you can climb back up from and course-correct.

You Can Always Go Down, But You Cannot Go Up!

It's true. If you price your products too low at the time of launch or at any point for that matter, it is virtually impossible to course-correct later on. A correction will mean losing your existing target customer base (if you have any) and having to find a whole new, more affluent one. It is virtually starting all over again.

On the other hand, if you launch a brand or collection too high and meet price resistance, you can test lower price points by introducing a promotion or a special offer. You never discount and move the item to "sale" and assume that it is not a good product.

By creating a promotion and lowering the price temporarily, you can maintain your original price positioning and test lower price levels.

A brand I worked with did just that. The founder set her prices based on the above formula but met resistance. When she offered a promotional discount of 25% to new customers, she would make more sales and gain better quality customers. Once we realised that this was the right target for the product, we looked to see how to make savings and gain back what we were losing in terms of margin.

Moving manufacturers was one option, which triggered the need for a larger volume of sales in order to meet the higher MOQs. Sourcing slightly lower prices raw materials and negotiating better prices due to a bigger buy was another lever we could pull. Ultimately, knowing that the lower price point was easier to sell at meant that we could safely re-work our sales forecasts and targets and adjust our marketing.

Pricing this way means you can always revert back to a higher level if you wish to, or make more sales and give greater satisfaction to customers who happily think they snagged a bargain.

Pricing is an intrinsic part of brand positioning. Just because something doesn't sell doesn't mean that the price is wrong. There are buyers for every product at the right price.

If your product(s) or collection is not selling, check if the product/market fit is correct before going into despair mode.

Does the product look like the price tag it carries?

Is it the economic climate that perhaps is temporarily choking your sales?

Assess everything and experiment before you get "trigger happy" and relegate something to the sale pile. I am a firm believer that having Sale events too often teaches your customers bad habits. They learn to wait for discounts and, more importantly, lowers the positioning of your brand. That is a slippery slope and one that is hard to get back up from.

Tax and Pricing

I spoke about how to address the issue of tax as part of chapter 1 – Business Basics. I suggest you revisit that chapter again, but whatever you do, be certain you do not forget that one day if you do well and your sales grow, you will have to register for tax and add the tax to your RRP prices. Make plans for accommodating this extra cost earlier on so you do not suffer later.

Imagine the power you can have over your brand and profits by simply understanding how to "play" with your numbers. The more you practise pricing and test your prices, the more you will learn about your target market, your customers and, of course, make more sales.

And who doesn't want more sales?

7

Marketing & PR

"The best marketing doesn't feel like marketing."

Tom Fishburne

Whether you like it or not, whether you believe me or not, I want you to understand one thing. The minute you have a business and a brand, your main job going forward is not of a designer, or CEO or any other title you may use to describe your role. Your main job is being a marketeer. Everything else comes after and is of lesser importance.

You may be the greatest of designers, but if you do not know how to market your brand at the beginning and/or have a great marketing team, later on, you will remain mediocre at best or lose your business at worst.

And vice versa, you can be truly mediocre, unoriginal and uninspiring, but if you know how to market what you have, be it your product, yourself, or your big promise, you will survive and thrive.

Great marketing is what propels brands to greatness. Yes, of course, it has to be supported ultimately by a good product to truly succeed, but even the greatest of products cannot survive without good marketing.

What is Marketing?

Marketing as an activity these days is not so simple to pin down or easy to describe. It spans from offline to online, from sales to advertising, from organic to paid. But when the strategy behind it is well done and the activities are well executed, it makes all the difference, and the results cannot be denied.

So, I will, as always, keep it simple and give you the foundation. You can jazz it up and complicate it later, but for now, I want to share with you the basics most brands skip and then wonder why it's not working, and others have more success.

Storytelling Magic

To be able to market well, you need to be able to connect to your target audience. Again, that is why, at the risk of sounding repetitive, knowing your target audience intimately is the key to success.

When you know what they like and what makes them click (literally click that button to go to your website, buy, join your email list etc.), you can market in such a way that your message reaches out to them. Your message has to connect with them emotionally and pull at their heartstrings (desire) or connect to logic (need). Regardless of which body part responds, you want the response to lead to a sale.

Many creatives are so involved in the process of creating the product that when it comes to marketing, they make the mistake of focusing on just marketing and selling the product via its features. On occasion, they may go into the benefits. The common mistake many make is that they approach it in a mechanical, unemotional way.

But what would your marketing look like if you were to do it in a way that informs, connects and results in action?

To start with, you need to realise two core things:

1. To work effectively, marketing needs to be consistently done. Layer upon layer, you need to stack up your efforts. Sometimes the results come fast, sometimes they take longer.
2. To be able to connect to your customers - present and future - you need to entice them. You need to wow them with stories and masterfully weave a marketing web around them until you capture them. The best way to do that is by telling them stories.

As humans, we all love to hear stories. Since being small children, we hear stories from which we learn. We tell stories to gain attention and attract, get out of trouble, and get what we want. We identify with people and situations based on stories we hear. So naturally, storytelling is one of the most powerful and underrated people-to-person connection tools. The best part is, it is free and available to all of us.

Only marketing your product and pointing a cyber finger to the "buy" button will not get you a sale. But grabbing and holding the attention of the right potential customer through the power of words and images is how you do it. So here are the five key information topics you must focus on when marketing.

Why Me? Why My Brand?

Most creative founders shy away from connecting personally to their ideal target customer. But the truth is that people buy from people. Founders have the power to make a brand appear more human.

Sometimes potential new customers will discover your brand via an interview in the press or on social media with you and check out your brand. Other times, they may hear someone tell a story about you and something that resonates with them connected to you, and that trail will lead to your brand. It is also common to discover a brand via an ad for their products or an image in a magazine. While the product may be nice, it may not be enough to make the viewer pull out their wallet and become a customer. But browsing on your website and reading more about you, seeing your press or testimonials may persuade them to buy.

So many of your sales will come in a roundabout way as a result of something else. Often that something else can be and should be YOU.

So much in fashion can be copied, but no one can copy you, so why not maximise that opportunity.

Your personality, passion, experience as a creative person, lifestyle and hobbies, all of this individually or together contribute to your brand and help browsers become customers.

If you are shy and think your life is boring, you're not alone. Many, including me, think so. But consider that what is most personal is most general too. In other words, I can see by myself that I follow many social media influencers and watch stories of their humdrum everyday lives. But I like it and feel like I know them. I would much rather spend money and support my virtual "friends" than someone I don't "know." I bet many of your customers will feel just the same if you let them into your world in however little or big way.

Why You (the customer)?

OK, this is an easy one so long as you know your customer. When you have done the work to define them well and know them intimately, it is easy to know what to say to make them respond and connect. Knowing them allows you to speak to them and show them you know and care for them.

When you speak to them in a relevant way and resonate with them, they will feel seen and heard. They will feel as if you are in their head and "get them," and a sense of loyalty to you and your brand will form in their subconscious mind.

In today's day and age, when we are more disconnected than ever from other people, when a short attention span permeates every area of life, feeling understood, cared for, seen and heard is a much sought after emotional commodity. Whether your product or brand solves a problem or fulfils a desire, the fact is once people get to know, like and trust your brand, they will want to be part of your brand and all the possible associations that come with it.

And when you know your customers well, you know exactly how to get them on board.

Why Now?

If not now, when? Of course you want their attention and business now. Tomorrow is too late.

Money likes speed, and the universe doesn't like procrastinators. Have you ever wondered how come if you have an idea for something but delay taking action on it, waiting for the right time when you can make it happen, how one day you see or hear someone else doing the very thing you thought of?

Ideas do not belong to just one person in the whole wide world. Ideas do not have owners until someone claims them.

Now, when your business is operational and you have products to sell is the only time when things have to happen.

Now is when people need solutions to their problems.

Now is the time to fulfil a desire.

Now is when your product is available at a certain price before it sells out.

Now is when you have a special offer or promotion running.

Now is when it is trendy to wear X and the right season for Y.

Are you with me? Can you see how when you are growing your brand, "now" is where we need to focus on and work from? Operating in the "now" creates many possibilities and, not to be underestimated, allows us to gather data and, based on that information, adjust our approach and fine-tune our strategies and tactics for maximum effect.

Why This (your brand/products)?

Most brands make the mistake of focusing on giving one-dimensional reasons why someone should buy this product offer.

Here is what I see a lot:

1. Products promoted off the back of a piece of the press or an image of an influencer with the said product.

2. Image of the product announced to be available for sale or presale at X price. Click here to buy.

3. Descriptions of the product and its features and composition as a reason to buy.

None of the above really result in many sales. They fall flat and do not connect to viewers and browsers. They lack emotional reasons to buy.

At a time when the fashion market is oversaturated, and it can be argued that not a single product needs to be manufactured and come onto the market as new, people need a reason to buy from one brand versus another. They like to be "courted" and seduced into buying.

Just because your product or brand is bigger, better, sustainable or … (insert words by which you describe your brand) is not enough of a reason for the majority of people to buy.

Competing on price is also not a strategy as there will always be someone cheaper than you.

What other brands cannot compete with is being different. They cannot compete with how you connect to your customers and how you make them feel.

When you focus on highlighting the benefits of the product and the obvious features, when you mix in some of your story, mission or vision, you give your customers more reasons to choose your brand and product over others.

Why should they buy your product? Tell them as if your life depends on it, like how you describe the things you love the most to others, with passion, with emotion, with stories that make them laugh or cry and fall in love with what you love, just like you. That's why they should buy your product!

Why No One Else (i.e. your competitors)?

If you want to make your competitors irrelevant, you need to act like they don't matter and tell your current and future customers why.

No one can be you, the brand founder. People buy from people at the end of the day, so tell your ideal target customers why no one else is like you. How are you different, what makes you special, tell your story and journey, and what matters to you.

People buy products when they want them or need them. Tell them how your products are better and different and what they have that others don't. Create that desire in your own way and in a way that your ideal customer will connect to. A sense of humour, a big heart and passion, or attitude and stance on something. Copycats can copy products but not sell them to the same audience the way you can.

People these days want to buy and even invest in purchasing from brands that they recognise themselves in. In other words, brands that support a higher cause are authentic and recognise the shortcomings of the fashion industry and try to offset them.

If you study your competitors well, you will recognise where they excel and what areas they lack. Pick up on their weaker points and brag about how your brand is better. Call out industry or other brand shortcomings and speak about how you are addressing the issues. Make other brands' weaknesses your strengths and make it known you are different and better. Those that care will come. Make it worth their while. Overdeliver and your competitors will not matter to your customers either.

Marketing Essentials

Now, while all of the above is important, knowing how to use it is essential. If you are the only one who knows how good your brand and products are and how no one else can compare, what use is that? Keeping quiet about it won't generate sales.

So you need to create some essential marketing assets and employ them to see the results you want.

Clear Messaging

At the core of all marketing is your message. Knowing what your message to your audience is and communicating this clearly, concisely, consistently and repeatedly across all channels and touchpoints is key.

As humans, we have the ability to see, hear and see. Effective marketers understand this and ensure a marketing campaign or even a simple message delivers the same message, notion, and idea on all three levels.

Successful marketers also focus on ONE thing at a time.

They decide on one core idea, product, or element they will promote within a marketing campaign and only deliver on it. Why? Because a confused mind always says "No." The human brain cannot cope with too much choice. It gets confused and cannot make a decision and, as a result, moves away from whatever is causing it to be in a state of overwhelm. If you put too many ideas, suggestions or call to action within one campaign, people will not know how to prioritise and rationalise to make a single choice or take a single action.

Let's see this in practice.

An amazing example to deconstruct is Nike.
The brand stands for speed, movement, power and motivation.
Their motto or brand strapline is "Just do it!"
Their swoosh logo has a sense of movement in the design.

As a brand, Nike doesn't care how old or young, heavy or slim or what gender you are. They want you to be happy and healthy and encourage you to "just do it," make a start no matter when, where and how. Just do it! Get moving.

The brand offers a wide range of garments and accessories in different sizes, colours, styles and designs to help you "just do it." Why? Because it will make you happy-ier and healthy-ier.

The advertising campaigns use successful sportsmen and regular people who, out of nowhere, have made a start and succeeded in something. No matter how small or large, their stories and achievements are inspirational, touching, and make us want to "just do it" too. Search online and see Nike's Unlimited Youth ad campaign featuring the Iron Nun - an 80+-year-old nun from the USA who started running in her fifties. Over the years, she ran multiple marathons and has finished a few Iron Men competitions too. Telling her story with a sense of humour is touching, inspiring and memorable.

Nike is successful because their core message of inspiring people to get going and improve themselves and their health is consistent no matter the year, the audience, the culture, the language, the demographic target market or state of religion, politics and economy. They never deviate from their message. Everything they do as a product offer, every piece of content seen or heard by people is on point and on-brand.

Why don't they offer diamond jewellery? Wouldn't someone maybe want to go for a run with a diamond tennis bracelet? Maybe. But diamond jewellery is not "on brand" and doesn't achieve their core brand mission of getting you to move. There are hundreds of products no doubt they think of and offer which can make them even more money, but they resist the temptation because, ultimately, they do not fulfil the brand's mission and vision. You get the point, right?

Lead generation

If your message is clear, you need to employ it in multiple ways across all possible channels and bring in potential new customers to your brand. In marketing, these potential customers are called "leads." Your brand needs to have a constant flow of leads in order to convert these to customers.

The process of utilising different methods to bring in leads to your eCommerce or bricks and mortar shop is called "lead generation."

Lead generation has the single objective to convert leads into customers.

The more leads you bring in, the more sales you will make.

The conversion percentage will vary from brand to brand and market to market, but one thing is certain. The more you know your customer and the clearer your message is, the higher the conversion percentage.

The Three Types Of Customer Leads To Nurture

When you are in lead generation mode, you need to consider that at any one time, you will be marketing to people who will be in one of three "market awareness" stages:

- People who have never heard of your brand or you – otherwise known as "cold" audience;
- People who have seen you but not yet bought anything – otherwise known as "warm" audience;
- People considered to be "hot" leads are those who know you, like your brand, trust you and are already customers.

Your marketing message, which we have already established, must be clear and focus on one core idea. It needs to be morphed in different ways to attract the right clients, who can be at one of the three levels of (your) brand awareness.

Future customers who have never heard of your brand perhaps will be attracted by the single image of your bestselling product. Maybe your brand story is told in a quirky way that will catch their attention and inspire them to google your brand for more info. Maybe it is a short post with an arresting statistic that will stop them from scrolling.

Ask yourself why those who are aware of your brand have not yet become customers?

What more do they need to see, hear, and feel to bridge the gap and spend with you?

Could it be some customer testimonials that will take away any nervousness they may have? Or perhaps some extra information on the benefits of shopping with your brand?

Your current customers, just because they already bought from you, is that enough? Or do you want them to buy again, and again, and again? Yes, I think so too. There is nothing better than a customer who knows, loves and trusts your brand and is ready to buy repeatedly. Just think of Apple, how they cultivated a loyal customer base ready and waiting to buy anything new they launch on the market. What would your customers need to buy more? (There is more on this topic in the next chapter, but for now, just get your imagination going.)

Study successful brands, and you will soon notice how they market to people from the three stages of brand awareness. Look up a successful brand that perhaps you are not following much and search for a product that they will appear in the search for. Click and browse and then notice how they target you through ads. Sign up for their newsletter and notice how they introduce you to their brand, communicate to you and when and how they make you an offer.

Successful brands that sell a lot and show continued growth are successful because they are **constantly, consistently and repeatedly** marketing to all three market awareness ideal customer profiles and move cold leads to warm, then hot and nurture them to remain as customers.

This process is not complicated nor just reserved for big brands, but it does require strategy and continuous execution.

Repel & Attract

The above process is even more effective when you increase the conversion percentage from cold leads to sales.

To do this, you need to know your target market well and have courage. Brave marketers create marketing posts and campaigns that polarise the audience and strongly attract the people who are the best fit for the brand, and repel those who are not a good fit. Often this is referred to as having a "marmite" effect. Have you ever met a person who kind of likes marmite? You probably never will either; people either love it or hate it.

Have you ever travelled out of your way to buy a vanilla ice cream? I haven't, but I can give you many examples of when I have travelled across town and spent a considerable amount of time getting to a particular ice cream shop so I can buy a particular flavour other ice cream brands do not offer.

Food and fashion have a lot in common. They offer an experience people are willing to go the extra mile for. The job of a good marketer is to craft a marketing vision that makes people go that extra mile, remember the product, want it more than another and need your product because it works better. Usually, this is achieved with marketing that is on point, hits the mark with your ideal customer and stands out.

Higher conversion percentages are achieved when you attract more of the right target customers and repel those who are not a great fit.

Omnipresence

Gone are the days when you asked where your ideal customers could be found; you were certain they could be found in one main place. Gone are the days when potential customers would see an advert for your product and buy it then and there.

At present, customers have more choices than ever and are surrounded by more noise than is good. What does that mean to you and for your brand?

According to marketers, our attention span is less than a goldfish (i.e. nine seconds) in today's day and age, and we are more cynical and mistrustful than ever. To remember something, we need to see it at least seven, 14, 21+ times (the number varies depending on who you listen to). Certainly more than a couple of times. And because people are wired differently, there are multiple social media channels, search engines, apps, shops and platforms that cater to every preference, taste and desire.

In plain English, to attract more leads, you need to work harder. You need to be everywhere at the same time. In other words, your brand ideally should be marketed across multiple channels where your ideal customers may be found. The more people that see your brand, the more they will come to recognise it. If your brand is well-aligned to who they are, eventually, they will become customers.

People who like something are more likely to try it. Matching people's expectations creates "trust." People who trust a brand are more likely to return and buy again.

Meeting people where they are and getting them to see your brand and products multiple times means you need to be seen to be everywhere. Being "everywhere" is not easy if you are a small brand and have a small or no team and marketing budget. Yet, it can be done. Let me show you how.

Content Repurposing

Most creatives understand the importance of marketing their brand and product. They try to do it but often inconsistently. The biggest reason for not often posting and across multiple platforms is the time and effort required. It can take a considerable amount of both, particularly if you do not have a strategy in place, and always try to develop new ideas.

To reduce both and for your marketing to be more effective, you need to understand how to leverage what you have. The best way to leverage it is to repurpose it. Here is how it can be done.

Let's say you have a new product that you are launching. You need to write to your audience, post across social media channels and advertise to announce the launch. Maybe, you'll need images and some written copy.

Because the information will broadly speak the same, I suggest you start with the one piece of content that can be used as the basis for everything else. Let's say your email to your subscribers or a press release.

The text and images you will use will be the same ones you can use to post on social media. With these content assets (text and images), you create a few variations of posts: single posts, carousels, quotable graphics, you can record an audio file of the text, you can animate the images with the text to become a small video, you can record yourself talking about the new launch, create short stories and reels etc.

You can use the same images and content to pitch to podcasters to be interviewed, pitch to the press and bloggers, and create advertising assets for promotional purposes.

As you can see, with one piece of content, you can slice it and dice it to become so much more without reinventing the wheel.

Of course, you should do a few different posts, cover the 5 WHYs and apply the same repurposing logic. Then you will have an abundant amount of content to share across all channels for a while.

You can automate the content to drip-feed it. While that is slowly releasing, you can be busy doing all the other important tasks a fashion brand founder needs to do.

I will be honest and tell you that it does take time to create content, even if you know what to do and the main piece of content is already created. But no one said you have to be the one to do it all. So, get your thinking hat on and figure out how and to whom you can delegate.

Traditional Marketing

Back in the day before the internet existed, traditional marketing relied heavily on print. The online marketing of today has moved focus somewhat away from traditional methods. However, I would argue, there is still a place for old-school marketing now more than ever.

As good and useful as online marketing is, you need to think and be reminded to go back to a particular website or web page. But when you print something like a leaflet, brochure or catalogue, you can reach people who may never come across you on the internet. You don't know in whose hands the printed material can end up, and it also can last longer than you can imagine.

Printing and sending look-books to magazine editors by post is something most millennials do not think of doing. But it can be very useful.

A few years ago, I got a phone call out of the blue asking me for a piece of jewellery to be couriered urgently to a well-known fashion publication. They found my brand through a printed look-book I had sent them years back, and they had filed away. Then when they were doing a story on astrological jewellery, one of my collections was a perfect fit.

Printing catalogues alone or collaborating together with other brands is a great way to raise your brand awareness. Small catalogues often are kept to one side to look at later. Especially around Christmas and birthdays, they are great for finding gift ideas. Some of the brands I know who do catalogues swear by how effective they are. Especially also with older customers who, unlike the younger generations, do not do everything online.

Catalogues, leaflets, and being featured in the printed press are also great. Many of those can grace the hotels and professional offices tables. Imagine having your product and brand featured in an inflight magazine. How many people who may not ever come across your brand can get to know about it?

Or what about dropping some leaflets or brochures about your brand in a few doctors waiting rooms if your ideal customer is someone with a specific medical problem. It doesn't get more targeted than that, right? If your brand is solving a particular problem that people keep quiet about, it will be hard for you to build online quickly a very niche target audience. Knowing where these people go for help and engineering the opportunity for them to come to see and know your product and brand is an important growth strategy for any brand.

Also - thinking outside the box a little - what about sponsoring an event and having your brand logo or product image printed on conference tickets or brochures?

There are many ways in which traditional print marketing can play an invaluable strategic part in the overall marketing strategy and plan. So don't ignore it.

Digital Marketing

Digital marketing, of course, is what everyone thinks about when the word "marketing" is mentioned. The great thing about digital marketing is that it is constantly evolving. Marketing online these days can involve written content, audio and video. It can be pre-recorded or done live in the spur of the moment. You can be the creator or pay someone to create it for you. You can do it daily or batch it and automate it to drip feed as and when you decide.

Digital marketing has allowed us all to be who we want to be without having to ask for permission. How big or small, visible or invisible you want to be, is up to you these days. You don't have to ask for favours or have a solid network to "make" it! You can BE anyone you want to BE!

You can be an author, a show host, a designer, a retailer, a model, a consultant, anything really. With or without a website, you have countless free platforms and avenues via which you can promote yourself or your products and brand. Your own website is a marketing tool. Posting on social media is marketing.

If writing is a skill you're good at, guest posting for other brands, blogs and magazines is a good way to market as it also helps with SEO. If you're not shy and comfortable with creating video content, the possibilities are endless.

What is important with so much choice is to be selective. Know where your ideal target customer can be found and be there. Be targeted and strategic, don't "spray and pray."

Because social media is evolving so fast, and with this evolution, we have new platforms coming through frequently, algorithms frequently changing with or without our knowledge, social media trends come and go. It is important to try to stay on top of what works and what doesn't. There are many social media companies whose job is to keep abreast of the news and trends and advise their followers on how to make the best of what's out there and available. Find these companies and find a few you like, and follow them. Be alert and informed. Spend a certain percentage of your time regularly reviewing and adjusting your marketing strategy to include and reflect changes taking place online.

When it comes to online marketing, you cannot afford to set it and forget it. Instead, you need to make it your job or hire someone who can stay informed, strategically filter through all the changes with your brand and business in mind, and tweak and adjust accordingly. Remember, as soon as you launch and have a business, your number one priority becomes marketing. Your number one overarching responsibility as an owner is marketing. The main hat you'll wear is the one of a marketer.

Email Marketing

A powerful and very under-utilised (by small to medium-sized brands) form of marketing in fashion is email marketing.

Imagine having at your fingertips access to many people who are your customers or interested to become one. Imagine knowing how to get in touch with them and tell them what you want them to know and hear. Imagine being able to subtly and gently influence their purchasing habits and become a trusted "friend." Imagine being able to select a certain group of people, just customers, or just new to your brand "friends" and send them a special message, a special offer, ask for their feedback.

Some of this you can do through social media, some you can't. But what happens if social media disappears? Changes algorithms, and no one sees your posts? If your account gets blocked or hacked?

The answer to all of the above and many other questions is owning the data. People saying "yes" to being on your email list are people who have raised a hand and, for one reason or another, shown interest. Given you permission to be in touch with them. Repeatedly!

Depending on the email marketing platform you use, you can create various segments of your list and, over time, know their interests, what they buy and how often, what they will like, who the big spenders and the bargain hunters are. Imagine what you can do with your data that doesn't depend on the whims and fancy algorithms.

Making email marketing a core part of your marketing strategy is a smart move big brands focus on and have whole teams dedicated to it. They study the data and use it to drive more sales.

Many small brands underestimate how powerful email marketing is and can be. They are scared that they will annoy people by emailing too much and getting unsubscribes. They fear that people will go off their brands and never buy again. Yet, big brands keep on bothering their subscribers and sending regular emails come rain or shine.

Why? Because they know that email marketing works. It gets people to buy. It gets people to talk. If anyone unsubscribes, they were once signed up to that list, which means they can be found online elsewhere through retargeting and tempted to re-subscribe again. It is not forbidden to join and leave an email list as often as you want to, right?

Instead of wondering where to find your would-be customers online, you can have them join your email list and communicate with them via their email inbox. They may not open every email you send them, but they will keep seeing your brand name regularly and in time when they need to buy a present, or treat themselves or can't ignore a problem any longer, who do you think they will think of? It should be your product and brand, yes? I certainly think so! A sure way to be in that position is to have a way into their email inbox.

Text Messaging

Another marketing method not much used in fashion is text messaging.

According to marketing statistics, the open rates for text messages is much, much higher than any other form of communication. Yet it is not really used by fashion brands as part of their marketing strategy.

While you may struggle to get many of your customers or potential new customers phone numbers - it is not impossible. Once you have them - use them carefully. Do not abuse the trust people have placed in you by giving you their personal number. But imagine how powerful your marketing can be if you advised a certain segment of your email list to a special offer in advance of everyone else finding out? Or sending a few of your best VIP customers a special discount or preview access and making them feel special?

There are many SaaS platforms that offer the service of sending message en masse - so it is worth looking up the best one for your brand and integrating this touch point as part of your marketing strategy.

Word Of Mouth Marketing

The best form of marketing, without a doubt and the hardest to achieve, is word of mouth marketing.

To fully work, it has to be genuine and not forced.

For it to be genuine, people have to LOVE what your brand stands for or what your product does for them.

How do you get to this point? Knowing your target market really well, your ideal customer and delivering a product and service above and beyond. Over-delivering on your promises. Often it is small touches that ordinary people do that touch others and make them be remembered.

For any brand that wants to be successful in the long term, focusing on product and customer service is vital, no matter how small or large.

Who you know, what you know, where you can be found or seen is all good and useful, but what really creates change and growth is what people say about your products or brand. Do they genuinely rave about it, or are they not fussed if your brand disappears tomorrow.

When people love a product, they create greater demand for it. When people can't stop talking about a brand or product, they create the FOMO effect - the fear of missing out. FOMO creates queues and frantic Google searches that get people writing about brands and products few had heard about. Wouldn't you want that to happen to your brand?

It may sound hard to achieve, but it is not that hard if you think about it. Work your way backwards by asking questions like, what would over-delivering on your promises look like? What would touch your customers, make you smile and post online about it, or send you an email or tell their friends? If everyone gives a five-star service to their clients, how can you deliver 7-star service? In fact, to help you, google the best five-star hotel and then google a 6 or 7-star hotel. There are a few around. Try to see what makes them have extra stars, and you'll see what makes people go the extra mile.

Another useful way is to read reviews for brands and products similar to yours. Especially the bad reviews. Read them and see what people like and hate. That, too, will give you clues as to what you can do to surpass expectations and get people talking about.

Customer Testimonials

Psychology plays a big role in business. Knowing how people think is a powerful tool available to each and every one of us. When you know the basics of human psychology, it is a way to know which levers to pull in order to get the results you want.

Most humans are wired to feel safe as part of a pack. How is this of use for you to know?

Knowing this means that you need to make people feel safe to make a choice because others before them did. They will be safe to take action if they choose, and by doing so, they will be part of a larger group of similar-minded people. People they want to be like or a tribe to be part of.

In fashion and business, testimonials do exactly that. One human alerts another that they are happy with something and others should follow them, and they can be happy together.

> **Using testimonials, particularly for new brands, is a powerful way to minimise the risk most people will feel at spending money with someone new and unknown to them.**

And let's face it, despite the world becoming smaller through the power of the internet, it is impossible to know everything and everyone. I am sure you, just like me, come across brands that you have never heard of, and yet you discover they have a huge following. Do you wonder how come you didn't know about them sooner? Were they hiding? Are you not using the internet in the right way?

Testimonials bridge the gap and are a perfect low-cost method to gain trust, reach more people and above all, bring in more sales.

Organic vs Paid Traffic

There are two types of traffic all businesses need in order to have customers. Organic Traffic is when people find your business naturally without you spending money. Paid traffic often is referred to as "pay to play." In other words, you must spend money for people to find your business.

Depending on what type of business you have, what products you sell, what brand awareness exists for your business, the conversion percentage of turning traffic into leads to customers will vary. Making a note of this percentage over time is important as it will allow you to calculate your "pay to play" budget later on when you decide to spend money on advertising.

Getting organic traffic of any significance these days is hard. It is not impossible, but it requires time and a lot of strategically planned and executed effort.

Paying for traffic, on the other hand, is easier. There are multiple ways to do this, and the possibilities increase with every passing month and year as new technological developments come onto the market.

Thriving businesses need both organic and paid traffic. Finding a balance that works for you and reflects your budget and strategy as a brand and business is important. There is no formula to follow. You need to find what works for your business, which may change as your business evolves. If you want to grow your business faster, you need to put more money into advertising. If you lack financial resources or don't believe in this approach, organic traffic takes longer to build and generate but perhaps will have longer longevity and bring in more loyal customers. There is no right and wrong.

Growing your fashion brand and business organically means that you need to invest in a solid SEO. Your website must reflect what technology is valued at the time when you operate your business. Currently, the norm is designing with mobile use first and then thinking about how the website will look and operate on a larger screen. Other factors such as page load speed, good quality referring backlinks and keyword strategy are also important factors in ranking your website high on the search engines. Ranking high is important as if you are not on page one of a search engine, you may never be seen and get traffic. Getting to page one takes strategically implemented actions. A bit of a vicious circle, really. Then networking and getting others to post, mention, speak and link to your website is important; keeping your content fresh, relevant and frequent is highly praised by the algorithms. Track what works and doesn't, tweak your effort and strategy, and adjust according to algorithm changes. Not an impossible task, but it really is a full-time job.

On the other hand, Paid traffic means knowing where your potential customers are and advertising on these platforms to ensure they see your brand and visit the page you want them to see and, hopefully, convert to take an action of your choice.

Advertising now can be done across almost all social media channels and networks. You can use a static post that performs well and turn it into an ad. Or you can create a new specific advert post. You can turn stories into ads, reels and videos. Whatever you think of, chances are you can create paid advertising with it.

When you advertise, you can target different types of audiences. You can decide who to target and where to target them in most cases. You can narrow down your audiences to a super-narrow niche and even re-target people who took a certain action in the past, such as watching a video on your website or social media channel for a certain time or percentage, who visited your site but didn't buy or abandoned a basket full of products. You can target your competitor audiences too. Just about anything you can think of, you can do with advertising.

If this wasn't enough, you could advertise on other peoples websites (if they accept advertising), you can sponsor shows and social media posts created by others, you can work with influencers and pay them for content. The possibilities are endless.

Social Media Channels vs Search Engines vs Market Places

But because "pay to play" can work out rather expensive, especially if you do not get it right, it is important to know the different high-level options.

You will be forgiven for thinking that all social media channels are the same. Unless you are deeply ingrained in marketing, there is no reason to know that some social media channels are better to invest your time and money in than others.

To start with, you should know that there are two main types of platforms. Social media channels and search engine platforms.

Facebook, Instagram, Twitter, LinkedIn, TikTok, Snapchat and many others are channels. Single closed social media networks. They have and are their own ecosystem. People go to them to post and engage with other like-minded people primarily, follow accounts they like and consume the content they post.

Then you have social media channels like YouTube and Pinterest that look like platforms, but they are, in fact, search engines. Like Google, Bing, Yahoo - these platforms are searchable, and people use them as a go-to place to search for information. They aggregate sources of information as well as allow for information to be posted on their platform and make it searchable.

The difference may be subtle at first glance, but it is a difference that makes a huge difference to a brand with money to invest in advertising. People who sit on these platforms usually have an active interest in finding a certain kind of information. This makes them more prone to taking action. Advertising here using keywords and terms people search for means there is a greater chance of your product or brand being seen by the right type of person who is more likely to convert to a customer.

While some social media channels are better than others, depending on your brand and product, search engines, on the whole, are a safer bet in comparison. You can pay to only show to the right person looking for something specific with the right intent, as opposed to paying to show up to someone browsing or using the platform for another reason, and your ad shows up just because they tick a few boxes your ad targets.

Another place not to be underestimated and used strategically are market places. Etsy, Amazon, eBay and many others are shopping platforms that also allow for in-platform advertising. Placing your product on a marketplace where people come with the intent to buy and paying to show up higher in the search rankings can not only lead to sales, but these sales will become subscribers on your email list. If you have the right systems in place, you can re-target these leads and turn them into repeat customers with higher-margin yields. Wouldn't that be nice, less work and more profit?

Knowing where to be and how much to invest in advertising is a strategic decision you need to take as a business. Starting small and experimenting until you find out what works, and only then increasing your spending, is the secret to a successful return on investment.

But make no mistake, if you want to seriously grow your business, sooner or later, you will have to invest in advertising. Knowing this in advance will allow you to prepare the ground for it. Advertising only works if you have a well-structured brand and your marketing assets are well aligned with each other and with your brand. This doesn't happen overnight and is one of the main reasons advertising doesn't work for some brands and can result in the waste of vast amount of money.

Getting Press For Your Brand

Last but not least, another form of marketing is generating press. The press plays an important part in brand positioning. Get the right piece of press, and your bank account will thank you. Or not.

Press can also come at a high cost if you don't know how it works and listen to industry "experts." So here is what you need to know and have as marketing assets in order to approach journalists and editors and get featured in the magazines.

You (DoItYourself) vs Them (DoneForYou)

Getting press is not rocket science. It requires either having the right network of contacts or putting in the time to build up connections. If you are a small brand on a tight budget and not too experienced with the industry, I suggest you start by doing your own press. You would learn a lot and save a lot of money. But it will cost you some time.

Getting press is not as easy as it sounds unless you are well connected or have a newsworthy product or an interesting angle on a not so newsworthy product. But not impossible either, obviously.

PR companies usually charge a monthly fee (that is never a small amount of money) for their services. What they don't tell you, however, is that for the money you pay, they allocate a tiny amount of their time to your account. They justify this by explaining that every time they meet editors and stylists, they showcase all their clients and their products, but this to me is not the same as focusing on your brand alone. They respond to what the editors are looking for, which is necessary. But they do not do enough looking for opportunities for features for their clients. It is more of a responsive rather than proactive service. Again, I emphasise, for the most part, I am sure there must be exceptions.

To get brands to become clients, PR agencies show press placements they have already achieved for current or past clients, but that by no means is a promise of what they can deliver for you and your brand.

And this is where the problem lies. They overpromise, wow you and later underdeliver. They never agree to deliver on targets nor, in the vast majority, work on a results-based basis. When you don't get what they promised, there is always an excuse and a reason, and often you are at the centre of it.

So, if you have the money to spare, why not? The little you get might be worth it and better than nothing. But if you don't have spare financial resources, then doing it yourself is the best way in the meantime. Today there are many online courses to teach you how to do it, online databases to give you access to contacts, or you can do it old school. One by one, you can find the print and online titles that best align with your brand, and by reading articles, select the names of the journalists, editors, assistant editors and stylists to approach and pitch to.

One timely tip for you is to do what's least expected. Most people aim to connect to the main editors and get ignored. That's the obvious choice. But who does the groundwork and has the editor's ear? The assistants, right? They are the ones most ignored and the ones who, in the future, will be the editors. So why not be more strategic, connect to them, make "friends" with them, and get your brand in the press that way? Or add this approach to any other strategies you decide to employ.

Doing your own press also has the advantage of gaining further insights into the industry, hearing first hand what is trendy and of interest, developing relationships that may open unexpected doors and the best part, these are your relationships and contacts. No one can leave the office or stop working with you and take them away.

Consumer (B2C) vs Trade (B2B)

When you are looking to get press for your brand, be clear on what kind of press you want. There are two main types – consumer and trade press.

Consumer press means Business to Customer (B2C). It means magazines, papers and blogs that your customers will read and be influenced by when it comes to shopping.

Trade press is Business to Business (B2B). These are printed or online publications that deliver information to other business owners, retailers and retail buyers and alert them to new brands, products and trends. They, in turn, make buying decisions that will affect their business and sales.

Unless you have a serious strategy on how to get into stores, perhaps B2B press is not so important to get as it is more niche. Most publications are not widely known by your would-be customers, so you can't exactly use the press features to position your brand on the market and gain authority.

Getting the right B2C press is key. Therefore making sure, if you choose to work with a PR agency, that they have the right contacts is vital.

I made this mistake in the past. As I was already working full time and yet wanted to grow my jewellery brand, I decided to take on a PR agency to do the work for me. I decided that I should go with an agency specialising in premium jewellery instead of just fashion to maximise the results. They would have the right contacts, I thought. I went with an agency whose CEO was an ex jewellery magazine editor. Over the eighteen months, I was with them, I got some press, but almost all of it was within trade publications. This was of little use to me since my jewellery was not a great fit for most boutiques at the time and I wasn't actively focused on getting retailers on board. At the time, I failed to realise that coming from a trade magazine background, the agency CEO would bring with her all her contacts from other trade magazines. That is where she would easily get her clients featured.

Another example is a jeweller friend I had at the time. She was with another agency, and her jewellery was at an entry price point compared to my brand. The agency she worked with had strong links to women's magazines. She got many press features and generated many sales as a result, but no matter how much she asked for a variety, she always got the same kind of press, in the same 2-3 publications and a long list of reasons why they couldn't get other titles.

Target Press List

So, don't make the mistake I made or my friend. Ask questions and look for a pattern. Have your target list of ideal publications ready on hand.

Compiling these for you or someone you bring on to help you get press is helpful as it focuses you to again think where you can find your ideal customer.

I often find that people aim at the big titles. Everyone wants to be in Vogue. But is your client really buying and reading that magazine? Because if they are not, what's the point of you neglecting the titles your clients read and trust when it comes to deciding where to spend their money.

That is not to say you should ignore it. If being featured in certain titles will add authority and validation to your brand, you should then go after these titles. Perhaps you can create an A and B list, and these press titles go on the B list.

Compiling an ideal list of target publications in print and online is also useful, so you keep track of who you contact. Who the people in the publication are, what they respond to, what they are working on, what intel you find on them that will help you to use as a connection tool - i.e. information that can help you open a conversation the next time you call or have an excuse to call again and then follow up with a business question.

Getting press may not be rocket science but getting the right press features requires a certain amount of strategy and networking. Any help you can get is not to be underestimated.

Stand Out To Be Noticed

What are the ways in which you can approach editors, bloggers and influencers?

Before the internet, people used to send letters. These days everyone sends an email. Often the emails can end up in the junk folder. Often emails look and sound the same. They all want the same. And so they get ignored and left unopened.

So how do you get noticed? What makes editors pick you and come back to you and be the first they think of when they need something?

Putting yourself in their shoes will help to answer this question. Imagine you receive hundreds of emails per day. Which will you pick to open? Perhaps one from a name of a person you know or recognise? Or maybe a catchy titled email, making it easy for you to know what the email is about? Once you open the email, do you want to read a long rambling email, or do you want to immediately see an image that will catch your attention or make you press the "delete" button?

Editors and fashion journalists often work to deadlines and need images, information, prices and whatnot "yesterday." Are you fast to respond? Do you have all at hand to reply quickly? Speed matters, and making it easy for them to do their job is the key to a fruitful and long-lasting relationship.

The fashion press also works on stories, and some stories are more seasonal and predictable than others. Knowing who will be writing about a topic and when their deadline will be, is essential. Some publications like glossy magazines have longer lead times, some as long as 4 months in advance. Others work on shorter lead times, like a month or a week. Make it your business to know how different publications work and when their deadlines are so you do not miss out if you stand a chance.

How do you find out? You can call and ask. Or you can search for this info on the relevant publication website. Usually, this type of info can be found in the Media Kit most publications have, and you can find a link to it in the footer of their websites.

Also, don't just rely on email. How else can you communicate? Just because we are used to email, it doesn't mean that snail mail is dead. Double down and send your pitch by ordinary post too. Imagine getting a letter that is not a bill or asking for payment of something. That would be memorable, right? Or sending a nice catalogue, a look-book and a copy of a well-written press release?

Basically, if you notice from all I have said so far, the trick is to be clear and of value. Make their job easier and easy for them to do their job and you will be remembered and rewarded for it.

Think outside the box, and if you don't hear back, follow up. Anyone who has experienced success with getting press will tell you that success lies in the follow-up. Pick up the phone and check they got your email. Call and then send an email.

Getting press is a numbers game and a contact sport. You have to interact, not take the "No's" personally and above all try, and try again. They need you as much as you need them. And when you get featured, say thank you. It's the little things that matter and people remember the most.

8

Routes To Market

"Sell them what they want - give them what they need."

Anonymous

Sales!
  The lifeblood to any business and a task often avoided by many creatives.

Since you can't have a business without sales, there's no point musing over why some hate it and how others excel at it. If you can't do it, find someone who can. It's that simple. Or learn how to.

Luckily, thanks to the internet, we have more options these days, so not all selling has to be done in person, especially by you - the brand founder. Unless you're good at it and love doing it.

In the past, most fashion brands generated sales via a wholesale model (i.e. selling to retail buyers in order to be stocked in other shops) or if they had the resources to open their own shop.

Today, that model still remains. Except the DTC route has more possibilities and has tipped the balance in its own favour. The explosion of countless new brands coming onto the market is largely due to the fact it is so easy to set up a virtual online eCommerce store.

The Future Is Omni Channel

Most start-ups and small brands operate by choice (or because they have no other choice) from this arena. Neither is right or wrong and having a mix of both, in my opinion, is the perfect model. But more of that later.

However, what is more exciting is that in today's day and age, we as creators have so many more opportunities to make money than just relying on our own eCommerce or wholesale sales.

The saying "Do what you love, love what you do" I used to find so contradictory. Often, for many creatives, doing what they love is all they want to do. But it is not providing them with the finances they need to live from. This was and is still the case for many fashion brand owners, creatives and designers. And how can you love what you do if you are stressed because you are not making enough to live from?

Thankfully technology has changed all that. In today's world, I firmly believe that you need to grow a fashion brand in a way that allows you to bring in revenue from multiple sources. Not just one or two - but many. Not all at the same time, of course, but knowing what's possible and learning from the start to think bigger and look for the opportunities will allow you to add more income sources over time.

This is particularly important when you see what an effect a pandemic can have on a business. If this recent pandemic had happened only 30 years ago, most fashion brands would have gone bankrupt. Instead, many found a way to survive, and many, in fact, thrived. Some were born out of the pandemic and grew faster due to the internet and its possibilities.

Core Retail Business Models

To be able to make the best of what is available as options, you need to know what's possible.

Since there are no rules and no fashion police in the fashion industry, just about anything you can think of is possible. You just need to know it's there for you to make use of or think of it and test the idea.

B2C (aka Business To Consumer)

Business to consumer or customer is the same as the DTC model adopted by almost all fashion businesses now.

You can have your own store from day one. It can be an actual physical, bricks and mortar shop or a virtual eCommerce website.

But you don't even need to have one to be in business. You can open up or take part in a pop-up shop online or offline. You can organise one yourself or for better results as part of a collaboration.

And if this doesn't appeal, you can just join online marketplaces like Etsy, Wolf&Badger, NOTHS and many others and start that way. Little or no upfront costs are charged to join.

Truly, access to customers has never been so easy.

You can also trade in person by going to markets. Also, getting others to sell on your behalf in exchange for a commission is a viable option.

There are other ideas you will discover as you open your eyes to the possibilities. The best part is, you don't have to pick and choose. You can start with any of the above and do it all if you want to.

Having multiple routes to market is essential as it allows for diversified sources of income and lowers the risk to your business. To do that, you must ensure you price your products with enough margin to allow for the commission to be paid, if necessary and still leave you with some profit.

B2B (aka Business To Business)

Depending on the type of brand you create and your products, you can also sell to other businesses.

You may launch a brand that solely caters to doing business with other businesses. *Corporate wear* is one such example. Many businesses require their staff to wear uniforms and are not in a position to manufacture their own. They have to buy them from somewhere, and often they need them to be designed to a certain specification and brand palette. The same can apply to accessories products.

Another interesting source of income that can work alongside a DTC business model is *corporate sales*. Many large businesses organise internal and external events that require them to give gifts to attendees or clients. They need to purchase those gifts from somewhere, right?

It is not something large brands, especially luxury brands, speak about, but many have actual teams of people generating and looking after corporate sales. Often large banks and financial institutions will have big budgets set aside for such marketing and promotional gifts. Their affluent customers will appreciate quality products, so for this reason, they would approach to work with premium brands.

Selling to corporations is not just reserved for large brands, but it does require some time to develop relationships. Aside from the better margin, corporate sales help add extra products in your manufacturing pipe, which can help negotiate better prices on the manufacture and raw materials.

Doing business with other businesses can have many positives. But, it does require some time to research and develop these relationships. Also, it is not a suitable option for every brand as corporate orders tend to be more specific and have rigid and conservative requirements in some cases.

But many fashion brands evolve over time. Sometimes, this evolution leads to opportunities that strengthen the business rather than weaken it. Many of these B2B opportunities go under the press radar and are not publicised, therefore not detrimental to a carefully crafted brand image.

Fashion Business Opportunities

Regardless of how you choose to do business, having multiple sources of revenue is important. It is best to have one or 2 main sources secured and working well before you begin to experiment and add on more diversification.

Many of the below-listed ideas present opportunities and benefits to brands. But often, they require additional planning and advanced strategies to be put in place. If you do not have your main source of revenue well established, adding more can distract you and end up being detrimental.

Wholesale

Selling to other retailers, of course, is the traditional and most common B2B route most fashion brands take.

This sales model is an important route, particularly for the more premium-priced and luxury brands. But going into wholesale requires product pricing that allows for it and a cohesive collection. Often brands learn the hard way what that means and what is required.

Another aspect of wholesale most new brand founders are often unaware of is that retail buyers watch brands for a few seasons before buying. Unless there is so much press surrounding a brand or product that acting fast and seizing the opportunity is a no brainer.

Wholesale buyers must consider their own efforts and customers before bringing a new brand onto their shop floor. They listen and watch before deciding and taking the "risk" to buy into a new brand.

Having a good reputation delivering on time, being professional, having a good sell-through rate, and a strong, engaged social media following are all selection criteria buyers consider when reviewing a brand.

Positive: Getting a few wholesale accounts as part of your sales and marketing strategy is a wise move. It helps with positioning your brand on the market. Particularly if you are a premium or luxury brand. Perception is reality, after all.

Being stocked in premium and luxury retail stores, having your products placed in proximity to well-established competitor brands speaks volumes to your target market. If they had never heard or seen your brand before, they will now. If they had ignored your brand before, they would become curious to know more now.

Being stocked in a well-profiled retailer helps with marketing too and often with the press. Many high-end stores treat their business as a brand, just like you, and work on generating press for themselves. Being stocked in such a shop means your chances of getting in the press increase immediately.

Being seen to be stocked in the right places can work wonders for your brand reputation and exposure. It adds an instant trust factor with your ideal customers.

Negative: But for all the positives, there are negative aspects that mustn't be ignored.

If you have not priced your products from the outset, knowing that you will want to go into wholesale, you may not be able to afford it.

I am of the opinion that when you are small and starting out, even if you don't have a generous profit margin allowing you to wholesale if an opportunity presents itself and you can get into an amazing retail store and not lose money (i.e. achieve break-even point) you should take the opportunity. But some brands do not even know what the break-even point is for them. Without this knowledge, they either say "No" and never perhaps get another chance again or say "Yes" and lose out, which ultimately can lead to all kinds of other problems.

Also, financial peril aside, reading the purchasing terms and conditions is vital. If you gloss over them, you may make extra stock at your cost and be stuck with it.

Agreeing on payment terms that are fair and work for both parties is essential. Retailers often want to buy stock and only pay a month or two post-delivery. While this payment arrangement is great for them, it rarely works favouring the creative brand since you must buy the raw materials, pay for the production and then wait for weeks and months before you get paid. Not to mention that many well-known retailers want to test a brand by offering an "opportunity" to be stocked on a consignment basis. In other words, you give the shop your products without agreed payment and only get paid if and when they sell something.

When I was wholesaling my jewellery brand, I had the opportunity to be stocked in one of London's best jewellery boutiques at the time. Prime location, multiple branches, my ideal customer was their clientele, and the owner loved my jewellery. Pinch me moment.

But she could only offer me on consignment terms, which after some consideration, I accepted. She over-ordered and soon returned half of what she had chosen, and I had especially made for her. She sold almost without fail every month, which was great. Except I had to chase for the sales reports, then for the payments. It then transpired that she wasn't always telling me what sold and what didn't. I made friends with the sales girls in order to keep a tab on the internal going-ons of the shops.

All in all, it took so much negative energy that, in the end, I pulled out as my sanity became more important to me than the sales. I still have leftover stock as a result. Luckily, I can melt the metal one day, but most brands making clothes and accessories cannot do that and will be out of pocket in a big way.

Of course, this is not how all retailers work, but also, it is not an isolated incident. I share this story, so you know not to go into these relationships with your eyes shut. Ask questions, trust your gut, read the small print and ensure you are clear on what the upside is for your business.

While not necessarily negative, many more aspects can lead to negative effects for a business. It's impossible to list them all and discuss them here now, but if you take away anything from this section of the book, let it be that the right wholesale relationship can be a game-changer for your fashion brand. But, you must start small and build on it gradually while staying alert and business savvy.

Pre-Sale / Kickstarter

In spring 2009, the Kickstarter platform was launched. With it, the concept of pre-selling something, getting money upfront to fund manufacturing and delivering the finished product to eagerly awaiting customers at a later promised date.

Since then, at the time of writing this, over 20 million people have backed all sorts of projects (not just fashion-related). Multiple billions of dollars have been pledged and successfully funded close to half a million projects. If that wasn't enough, the term "kickstart" has become synonymous with the idea of pre-selling a product or service.

In fashion, where costs are high, timelines long, decisions often based on emotions and not data and problems easily occur and even more easily turned into costly mistakes, offering products and collections on a pre-sell basis has been undoubtedly revolutionary.

Not only have mistakes been spared, but the pre-sale model ties in nicely with the sustainability movement and drive towards less consumption and more considerate purchasing.

Positive: The positives are obvious. A brand, particularly those new to the industry, can use this business model to validate an idea. Offering a range of products on a pre-sale basis allows them to see what is more commercial. It captures the desire of the potential customers versus what doesn't.

I cannot tell you the countless times when working for a brand, we will take internal bets as to what will be the best seller from a new collection, and most of us will be the losers time and time again. Often, what we see as appealing, amazing, revolutionary, must-have and more, is not perceived in the same way by the actual customers. Perhaps the idea is not communicated well. Perhaps the design doesn't have photo and hanger appeal. Whatever the reason, if you go into manufacturing and commit to a production MOQ, brands will be sitting on a lot more unsold stock than if they took the time to validate their assumption and enthusiasm.

Also, it should not be underestimated what having money ready to pay for manufacturing can do. Especially if you sell more than your target. With bigger orders, you can take the opportunity to renegotiate your cost prices where possible.

Another positive is the raised visibility your brand will receive due to the extra marketing activities you will need to do to turn browsers into customers.

Negative: On the other hand, doing a Kickstarter campaign or launching products on your own website for pre-sell is not completely cost-free. You still have to photograph your products so you can market them. You need to invest a large chunk of time in strategically promoting the pre-sale and ensuring you adapt your approach if necessary, overcome objections, and perhaps offer discounts to sweeten the deal.

For smaller brands and businesses who do not have enough resources to rely on for support, these activities can take the eye off the proverbial ball and lead to loss elsewhere in the business.

Also, if a mistake was to occur during manufacturing, this can be costly to correct.

A brand founder I know some years back launched an activewear garment via a Kickstarter campaign. The campaign went better than expected, and she sold more than her target. So far, so good.

However, when it came to manufacturing, certain mistakes were made. There was no quality assurance process set up, and some "small design improvements" were made before production. Since no new samples were made to test the product's functionality prior to production, hundreds of units were made and delivered to the founder, which had a defect in them. The garment was not fit for purpose. Long story short, she spent a lot more of her own cash to remake the product again and, in the process, had to change her raw materials supplier and find a new factory to manufacture. Basically, she had to do it all over again to save face and reputation. And as far as I am aware, the brand never "launched."

So, as always, pre-selling is a great business model, but it needs to be planned well and executed even better. Depending on how you want to grow your brand, this can be how you launch and sell your collections, or it can play a key part in your overall business growth strategy.

Sell On-Demand

The "sell on-demand" model is something that has always existed in fashion. Selling couture garments is a form of it. Offering to make bespoke products is also a variation of the idea.

But in recent years, we have seen a new variation emerge, where brands offer products permanently on their eCommerce shop that are only made when a customer purchases.

Some brands, like Nike, offer this model as part of a personalisation program for a single product design.

Others offer more than one product for sale but advise that delivery will take longer as the product will only be made once it has been bought.

Positive: It is a clever "slow fashion" way to grow a business. It carries little risk for financial strain and exposure. It means you can manage the workflow. In theory, manufacturing on-demand means that you can purchase just enough raw materials as and when you need them, thus not tying invaluable money into stock.

It also makes for a good marketing story, as it taps into the idea that as a brand, you are ethical, sustainable and support a more conscious form of consumerism.

Negative: But on the other hand, the little risk it carries can come at a high price.

It is manageable to fulfil orders as they come, so long as you are the designer and maker of the products. But while you are busy making products, you won't be running and growing your business.

If you were to rely on outsourcing the making of the product, it might get tricky to promise delivery dates unless you can pre-book manufacturing time in advance. To work around this challenge, you must consider employing your own makers. But then you must keep them occupied every day since you'll be paying them.

Finding a factory to make on-demand is hard. As we established earlier, factories make money from larger production runs. If they make one-off pieces, they charge substantially more for it. Unless you have a factory you already manufacture a lot with, and they are willing to create an add-on facility to fulfil such on-demand orders. Most factories will not agree to manufacture on-demand unless they can charge extra and treat the single orders as sampling.

Also, manufacturing on-demand means higher costs. Buying small amounts of raw materials is costlier. Making one at a time is costlier. Shipping one at a time is costlier.

I'm not telling you this to put you off, but instead, so you know in advance what you will have to consider. You'll need to figure out a realistic plan to make it work and make a profit. Or not make a profit but make other gains that will push your brand and business forward.

Affiliates

The affiliate sales model is an old one that has been recently given a new spin. Technology advancements have made it even easier these days to get others to sell on your behalf and earn some money for themselves in the process. Low cost, high gains model.

Amazon has affiliate programs among many other large retailers and marketplaces. Anyone who buys via a personalised link will earn a small commission in return. SaaS companies, selling services and digital products, often rely on affiliates to promote and sell their products.

The same principle can now be applied to fashion. There are various ways in which this can be achieved. Software options are available to help set up the process of getting others to promote your products and make a commission every time a sale of your product is made.

Using this affiliate sales model is a genius way to add additional income streams to your business at almost no cost.

Positive: All it would require is a little time and perhaps a small cost upfront to set it up. Once set up, you have everything to gain.

You can train people on how to sell your products and incentivise them on how to sell more. The sky's the limit so long as you have imagination and willingness to invest your time in growing this income stream.

Negative: There aren't many negatives to speak of, but perhaps things to be aware of and keep an eye on.

Stock levels come top of the list. If you get people to promote and drive sales for your products, you must make sure you have enough stock to fulfil the orders and a stock replenishing plan.

Also, you must make sure your COGs costs and profit margins are accurate so that when you pay sales commissions, you are still left in profit.

Marketplaces

Joining marketplaces is a great opportunity for small and emerging brands to gain greater exposure and drive more sales. But with so many popping up all the time, how do you know what a good one to take part in is? All marketplaces are not equal, that's for sure.

Positive: The larger marketplaces like Etsy, eBay, NotOnTheHighStreet, Amazon and the like may not be suitable for all brands, particularly those aiming at a premium market positioning. But they are so well known and such popular destinations for shoppers ready to purchase that it makes no sense to ignore the part they can play in the growth strategy of some brands.

Not only do they have millions of visitors come to their platforms, but they have the training to teach you how to present your product and page in a way that will attract more visitors, rank higher in the search and more. All useful skills and knowledge that you can apply to your own website.

With the small fee they take in exchange for having your brand on their platform and bringing buyers to your store, they offer a lot more in return. Opportunities such as taking part in mailer campaigns, advertising opportunities, and in-person events, even some offer products to corporates.

Negative: But as with most things, for every positive, there is a negative or something to be aware of.

There are a few key areas to keep an eye on and remain business savvy about regarding marketplaces.

Most marketplaces help you sell the product but once sold, it is your responsibility to ship it. This is called "*drop-shipping,*" and the shipping costs can be hard to determine or fixed by the marketplace. You need to make sure you know what these costs will be and ensure you do not end up out of pocket.

Refunds are another aspect to be aware of and check what T&Cs the marketplace promises to its customers. How and when can customers return stock, and how and when do you get charged? Who covers the shipping back costs? Can you opt-out from accepting returns?

Some newer marketplaces that pop up approach emerging brands knowing they are desperate to be more visible and need sales. But truth be told, the new marketplace founders are in the same position as the young brands. In trying to get them to join, the marketplace founders or marketing teams paint a pretty vision of increased exposure and sales for the brands who join. In return (all!) they ask of you, the brand, is to market the marketplace in order to help bring in users and generate sales. That is a sneaky tactic, and if you do not use your common sense and you are not business savvy, you will soon be promoting someone else's business, bringing in customers that may not spend money with you, and if and when you make a sale, you still have to pay a commission.

Also, despite joining the marketplace, you have no way, as far as I am aware, to have access to the data of people who visit your product listing store page. It is not an insignificant issue, but perhaps there are clever ways you can think of to attract people not only to buy but in the process join (even if they do not become customers) your email list and retarget and re-market to them that way.

Collaborations

A great new way to grow your brand and business that is not new but has been revived during and post the pandemic have been brand collaborations.

Finding well-aligned brands but not in competition with yours is a great way to get double the results and more sales while also effortlessly (almost) expanding your brand visibility and exposure to new ideal clients.

There are many, many examples of successful fashion collaborations at any market level.

Some notable ones you might recognise are H & M collaborating with luxury designer brands such as Karl Lagerfeld, Moschino, Kenzo, Lanvin, Gianbattista Valli and many more.

Others are Ugg boots and Jimmy Choo, Dior and Nike, Louis Vuitton and the NBA (The National Basketball Association, USA) and countless more. Then there are collaborations brands often make with celebrities and influencers.

Positive: Where to start, there are so many.

If you pick a similar but different brand with the same ideal target market, then doing something together and promoting the collaboration jointly exposes both brands to a whole new group of potential customers.

Good collaborations grow your brand visibility and generate sales as a result and can establish your brand's authority on the market. It can act as a positioning lever if used strategically.

Some collaborations also come with a paycheque. In other words, as a designer brand, you might get approached to form a collaboration with a bigger company that can afford to pay you, as having your name next to theirs will create much-needed expansion and draw attention.

An example of this is a British designer Roksanda Ilinčić who announced a collaboration with a luxury property development firm some time back. An opportunity for her to venture into interiors and be exposed to a whole new ideal customer audience and for them to get coverage in the press, which otherwise they would have struggled to get on their own.

When I was working for luxury goods brand Smythson, we regularly collaborated with up and coming British fashion designers in order to keep the annual diary category alive. In a fast-paced new world where paper diaries were considered a thing of the past and replaced by the functionality of smartphones, keeping an iconic product alive was important to the brand. If we couldn't make the sales grow, we hoped to at least keep them flat and not declining. One way to do that was to collaborate with popular fashion designers at the time. We used some of their artwork to place in the covers of the diaries, agreed on a revenue model that worked for both parties and both were then invested in the promotion of this new product. A win-win for both sides.

Negative: A lot can go wrong with collaborations too. Not all is plain sailing. If the brands collaborating are not well aligned, they will not get much out of the effort they will put in.

If a clear and strong agreement is not in place, the whole collaboration may turn into a nightmare and even erode any gains made.

If there is no strategy in place, many products may be created and then left unsold.

As always and with everything, having a good strategy, putting a clear plan in place, and precise execution is the key to success.

Automated Upsell / Down Sell

Last but not least, upsells and down sells are an additional source of revenue, often underutilised by brands.

If you have structured your collection properly, in a cohesive way and also priced it as per the pyramid method we discussed in chapter five, you should have opportunities to offer your customers the chance to add to the shopping basket something else and spend more with you.

Or if they don't buy anything, perhaps in a follow-up email marketing campaign, you can offer them something less or more expensive and see what strikes a chord and makes them buy?

Many small brands are so focused on getting THE sale they miss out on spotting the many other opportunities available that can generate even more sales and turn one time customers into repeat ones.

When designing your website or checkout, design it so that you can offer more than what is in the basket.

When you thank a customer for a purchase, suggest something else that may be of value to them and perhaps offer them a promo code.

If someone abandons their basket, follow up and see if you can bring them back and convert them, if not with what they intended to buy but with something else.

If this sounds like an advanced strategy, perhaps it is. You need to have the basics in place to get to offering upsells and down sells, but knowing what's possible and working backwards is how you'll get to maximise your sales, nurture a loyal customer base and grow your business at the same time.

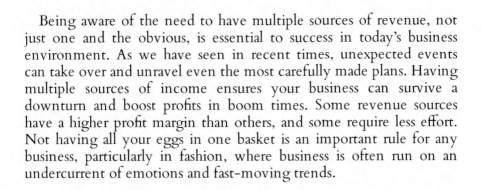

Being aware of the need to have multiple sources of revenue, not just one and the obvious, is essential to success in today's business environment. As we have seen in recent times, unexpected events can take over and unravel even the most carefully made plans. Having multiple sources of income ensures your business can survive a downturn and boost profits in boom times. Some revenue sources have a higher profit margin than others, and some require less effort. Not having all your eggs in one basket is an important rule for any business, particularly in fashion, where business is often run on an undercurrent of emotions and fast-moving trends.

9

To Launch Or Not To Launch

"Good fortune is what happens when opportunity meets with planning."

Thomas Edison

Day One Or...

Launching a brand, a collection or even a single product requires time, effort and money.

We are so used to hearing success stories of amazing launches that immediately upon launch sell out and "set the world on fire" that you would be forgiven for expecting that, when it is your turn, you'll get the same newsworthy reception.

Often, in fact, the reality is quite the opposite.

One of the biggest shocks new start-up creative entrepreneurs have is when they "launch" for the first time and realise that no one noticed.

No sales come immediately. No one wants to cover the monumental news or your "launch." No one and nothing pauses even for a second because your website went live and because you had decided, that on that day of all days, will be your launch. The servers don't crash under the (lack of) strain of traffic rush to your website. The bank doesn't freeze your account, thinking someone hacked it and is money laundering.

None. Of. This. Happens!

This can be upsetting and quite rightly so. After all the hard work, everyone wants to be recognised even a little bit.

I often have these conversations and tell entrepreneurs that all the hard work they put into up until that point was easy compared to what's yet to come. The hard work starts when your brand, collection or product is ready to be shown to the world.

To get to success, you need mental, emotional and financial stamina and to persevere.

You have to work on marketing to your target market. Making "noise" about it and selling it.

It can be argued that the journey of product creation, to a large degree, is within the comfort zone for most creatives. It certainly feels this way for me. I have no fear of creating any product. But I, like many of you, no doubt, have a lot of stories and fears about other necessary tasks required in growing a business.

The act of launching (and everything necessary that comes after) often requires us to stretch ourselves outside of our comfort zone (by a lot!) and develop new skills, evolve our mindset and grow as people in order to see the results we are so used to reading about and believe we deserve.

Launch vs Going Live

The main reason for "launches" going wrong and for entrepreneurs not always getting the reaction they want when they launch something new, I strongly believe, lies in the misuse of the word "launch."

In my opinion, most newcomers do not "launch" but instead "Go Live" with their project, brand, website, whatever new they are doing and finally revealing to the outside world. Unless... I will tell you later on of the exceptions.

Go Live

When you are just starting out and have spent months, and years even, working on something new, most people focus on just getting that one project to the finish line, to a point where it is "perfect" and presentable. In fact, more than presentable. Most people fear being judged, so getting their product or brand to be "perfect" is vitally important, and all effort is centred on this one very task.

Getting to the point where you can reveal your product to the world is a rollercoaster involving many trials and tribulations.

While many attempt to build a following, many start and stop by creating a few pages across a few social media channels. They do not formulate a strategy, post regularly, or work actively on building their community and fanbase. So when the big reveal day comes, there is no one to reveal it to.

Gone are the days when people had the mental capacity to notice newness in such a way that it elicited a response. Today's online world is too noisy. We are bombarded with so much information and events happening that we don't notice or care unless we have an active interest in it.

Our websites' search engines take a while to index websites and start showing them in searches. That is, if your website was built correctly and has the correct keywords used throughout the copy.

Social media profiles on various platforms where your ideal clients might be found take a while to build up and get enough followers. When you post, many will see your posts and engage with your content without buying.

Often creatives rely on eCommerce platforms for the building of their websites. They buy a theme and almost like "paint by numbers" replace as indicated the generic holding images with their own and add some copy. But that is by far not enough. Yes, your websites need to look great, but they also need to be technically designed and operate way better than you realise.

If you have not built up an email list by that point, then who will you be alerted to your "launch?"

A launch plan without a strategy behind it is called a dream. A half baked strategy based on hoping and wishing is not a strategy.

But there is a lot of positive to be said about Going Live and NOT launching.

You can call it a "soft launch" instead and delight in the fact that never again will you have this quiet time to be unnoticed and test things.

Ask a few people to test the buying process. Ask them to give you feedback on the customer experience of the website. Check the speed and other vital statistics that are key to a healthy eCommerce shop and criteria for a high search engine ranking. There is nothing worse than to have people waiting for the Go Live moment and your website is too slow to load or crashes, and whatever else can go wrong with it.

Remember, people have short attention spans. Once they try something and it doesn't work as expected, their attention moves elsewhere. There are plenty of other eCommerce shops they can go to, to distract themselves or spend their money.

Going live as a business quietly allows for an opportunity to get closer to the illusion of perfection. It is like the quiet moment before the storm.

Managing Expectations

Going live usually feels like an anti-climax. It allows imposter syndrome feelings to come to the surface. If there is a time to have your inner voice talk negatively and tell you how badly you've done, this is the moment. When you are tired and not getting what you expected.

Reframing the situation here is key. Managing your own expectations is a vital component of being a creative entrepreneur. It is a must-have skill if you are in fashion and plan to launch anything of your own.

I know it is easier said than done, but detaching from the outcome is a necessity. Not a "nice to have" skill. The fashion industry is fickle and wonderful at the same time. Anything you choose to tell yourself is just one of many stories. Be kind to yourself and pick a different, more supportive and kinder story to hear and believe in.

Whether you go live quietly, soft launch to just friends and family or launch with a bang, it does not determine the success of your brand in the long term.

In fact, it means nothing. As harsh as this may sound to some, it is better to have less success at this point, so you realise what you need to do to get the reaction you wanted. It is infinitely better than resting on an initial success (which almost always, by the way, is temporary) and later wondering why it didn't last and what went wrong?

What matters most is the steps you take once you reveal your products to the world.

What matters is that you do not run out of energy and steam just now, when you need it most. When you are just getting started!

If you flatline at this point, it will only get harder for you to pick up the pieces and reframe them later.

Launch

In all fairness, if you look at brands that launch successfully, you will notice that usually they are bigger, have an established audience, and have worked on a launch plan for months in advance. They have people dedicated to planning the launch, executing that plan, and overseeing the plan. They also have some, if not a lot, financial resources or connections which contribute in alternative ways instead of cold cash (aka sponsors).

You might think it is not just big brands that launch successfully. That smaller brands, start-ups and single founders can and have also launched with great success. It is true, there are those examples too. But they are few and far between.

For one reason or another, these creative entrepreneurial unicorns have something that has captured the imagination of the press and those who create the hype. It could be an amazing talent, or it could be the protege of someone influential. Fortunately or not, I have been in the fashion industry long enough to have seen many such "success stories" come and go like a flash in the pan.

There is no such thing as an overnight success. Pick anyone you admire and do a search on them, and undoubtedly you will find information to prove me right. Lasting success stories are founded on substance, good strategy, and even better execution They took years before they became overnight success stories.

... One Day

So what if you are working towards a launch? What if your past "launches" weren't perfect, but you want to get better and have the results and attention you read about?

Let's take a look at what you can do, in practical terms, so you launch rather than quietly Go Live unnoticed.

Just because you "launch" it doesn't mean it has to be on the very first day people see your brand or products. Launches can be made at a later date after you have switched your website on and started trading. You can launch a new brand, products, collections or services sometime after they are, in fact, ready. You can launch seasonal collections or limited edition runs or re-launch something because you have updated it or are celebrating a milestone.

Launches are not limited to something new and only to the start-up stages.

Usually, most people think of a launch as the actual event that takes place on a certain date, but that is a mistake. Launches have three core parts to them. Pre-launch, the actual launch phase, which can take longer than a day and post-launch activities.

It should also be remembered that launch events should be planned around two types of attendees: your existing customer base and followers and those that can help promote your product. This usually means the media, influencers, or industry experts.

Both play a huge part in making the event a success, and that's why it is a good idea to make it exclusive and special.

Your product launch event ideas should, first and foremost, be informational and educational at their core. Leave guests with a lasting memory and an excuse to talk about the event across social media. Also remember that it's always good to entertain as well.

Hence planning is crucial if you want to see great results.

Pre-Launch

Once you have decided on the purpose for the launch and on the "How," list out all the details and work out a realistic (add and include some buffer) timeline backwards. You will have an idea of the time needed to plan and execute.

Usually, depending on how important it will be, launches can take a few weeks or months of preparation. Especially if a venue needs to be booked, guest list agreed upon, gift bags planned out, sponsors found, project manager and teams put together, invites and other marketing collateral designed, printed, sent etc. You get the idea. There is a lot that goes into a launch from an organisational point of view.

Creating a critical path, similar to the one you create as part of managing the creative process and manufacturing, will help you be better organised, track all you have to do and not feel like you are spiralling out of control and fire-fighting all day long.

Then there is the marketing side of things relating to a launch.

You need to plan strategically what information will be communicated and when, how, and by whom.

There are three main reasons why a launch marketing plan should be created early in the planning cycle:

1.   A successful launch drives excitement, interest and brings in sales for existing products. It also brings in new customers and future would-be customers, prospects, fans, and referrals who can begin their journey towards conversion to purchase.

2.   Driving consumer demand in advance of a product coming to the market creates a "pull effect" by encouraging future and present customers to start asking for the product and retailers to pre-order, thus "pulling" the product through their distribution channels.

3.   Last but not least, it allows for the brand to develop a product narrative early. This, in turn, could not only drive the marketing strategy and plan, but it may also influence design or manufacturing.

As part of marketing, you need to make sure that you have people on stand by, ready to support you and amplify your marketing efforts.

It is important to plan how hype will be created and how the build-up to the actual main event day will be orchestrated. I say "orchestrated" as it takes a team or a small village to create buzz and excitement, let alone to maintain it. For maximum effect, the culmination of activities needs to be "just so" timed, not too early and not too late.

Teasing the launch date can significantly contribute to the buzz, "pull effect," and drive consumer anticipation as part of the plan.

To spread the word to maximum effect, it is helpful to have a PR agency and event organisers working on your launch project. Investing money in paid advertising, too, can work wonders if done right.

But if you do not have the financial resources for all of it or parts of it, you need to do something organic.

So think outside the box. Do something unexpected. Research unusual launches across any industry, see what ideas you'll get, and do your own interpretation for fashion.

Because it is easier to work to a formula, I often work to and advise the creatives I work with to aim for the 1-10-100 formula.

As part of preparations for the launch, make a list and pre-agree the support of the following:

1 (mini) influencer. The larger ones may ask for payment and be less effective, so make sure whoever you contact and speak to you

have checked out and is a great fit (i.e. has the right target audience for your products) for your brand. If you snag more than one, all the better!

10 (ideal client fit) people, press contacts, or writers at preferred publications who can email at least 10 people from their network about your launch.

100 friends and family who can spread the word to their friends and family, post about it etc. Aim for a hundred, and don't panic if you can't get the exact number.

You can elaborate on this formula by following the same rationale for, say, marketing. You can pick one topic, create 10 images, and create 100 posts to be used as part of your pre-launch campaign.

The idea here is that if you, at least, have this much pre-planned, pre-agreed and put in place, you will gain traction in the run-up to the launch.

To maximise the effort, create content that you can offer to people to use. What stops most people from supporting others is not knowing what to say. Or if left up to them, don't be upset if it is not the right kind of message they put out. So, take control and manage the outcome you want.

Creating a launch waitlist or countdown is a tried-and-tested method for building excitement around launches. Exclusivity and scarcity are great drivers of FOMO and popular tools for creating a sense of anticipation.

When the now-famous fashion platform Modus Operandi launched some years back, they created excitement and a real sense of FOMO by opening up a waitlist. Given the nature of their launch, they were taking pre-order of garments shown straight after their launch catwalk shows. Everyone and anyone who loved fashion wanted to have the chance to buy catwalk pieces and have them delivered at the same time as the shops were going to get their deliveries of the new season collection. But access was limited only to those who applied and were approved. This generated much hype and frenzy.

The scarcity and exclusivity technique is not new nor just limited to the world of fashion. A recent new social media platform was launched by only launching to Apple iPhone users and only by invitation. Once accepted, new members could invite up to three contacts from their contact list, which, of course, had to be Apple iPhone users. Given that the platform boasted the presence of celebrities and the ability to be in a virtual room with them and chat in real-time and live with the real celebrities, the FOMO factor was at an all-time high.

So creating interest and building anticipation is vital to the success of a launch and requires meticulous planning. But also requires you to know your target audience well, understand human nature and what drives and excites them, and think of original, bold ideas.

Launch

The more you organise in advance, the less stressed you will be at the launch itself.

These days you can have in-person launch events and also virtual launches. Which one works better depends largely on the type of brand you are and your target audience. But I would suggest that it is best to plan for both in today's day and age, where most brands from the get-go can have or even have a global audience.

A virtual launch allows you to be in many places around the world simultaneously or on the same day. It allows you to get guests, who may be too busy to travel, to pop in and show up in support. The lower costs allow for extra money to be spent in perhaps prize draws or any other activities that will get people into a frenzy and create the much needed social media buzz.

The advantages of an in-person event, of course, are unique in their own right.

By inviting select guests, existing and future customers, you're giving people the opportunity to experience, touch, and feel the product in real-time, in person, in a live environment. Not only is this an invaluable experience for the guests, but they also get to know the brand and the people behind the brand better. This, in turn, drives higher conversion rates of purchase consideration and can increase the word-of-mouth buzz across social media channels.

Successful in-person launches often incorporate an entertainment element. The options for event entertainment are many, so ensure you've done your research and, ideally, seen first-hand the act you'll consider booking.

It is essential to make sure that the type of entertainment chosen needs to align with your company's brand values and product narrative and your audience's expectations. Living up to and managing expectations often defines the outcome of an event, so don't leave anything to chance.

Last but not least, don't forget that launch events, whether online or offline, are all about the experience they create. When you create an experiential event, you are more likely to build brand loyalty and positive product sentiment.

Post Launch Reality

Many make the mistake of thinking once the launch is over, it is over. Wrong!

Like launching a brand or a collection, the truth is that once you have a launch, its success then lies in the follow-up effort. Sales are rarely made on the day. Sales come as an aftereffect of the launch event.

A great marketing plan for a launch will have an equally detailed post-launch plan, as it did for the pre-launch.

A great marketing planner will also recognise the opportunity to indirectly lift the sales of other products and categories due to the attention garnered around the launch. As a popular saying goes, "a high tide raises all ships." The same effect can be achieved with your launch too.

Often launches in fashion can result in appointments with buyers and clients. New press opportunities can open up as well as ideas and offers for collaborations. So be ready for these opportunities. You might not get another chance.

When you successfully build social media hype for your launch, you can and must try to keep this energy going for as long as possible after the launch event. Post your favourite photos from the event and repost pictures from your guests. Ask them to use specially created hashtags (perhaps the same as one used during the pre-launch phase) and ask them to tag your social media channels so you don't miss an opportunity to see, comment and repost such posts. High engagement fires up the algorithms on all social media platforms, and your account and posts get higher visibility.

There are many ways in which you can amplify the success of a launch. Equally, if a launch didn't go too well (or not at all), you have a chance to analyse why not and what went wrong and take fast action to address the issues. While these incidents may be painful, in retrospect, they are often game-changers. They help you understand your brand, product and market better than any research you'll do. If you manage to course-correct at such a time and find your way back, the success you'll find will be longer-lasting.

Last but not least, here is what you must do regardless of the outcome.

Celebrate!

Recognise how far you have come, together with your team of makers, freelancers, fans and supporters. Celebrate with them, show gratitude for your achievement. In fashion, there is so much focus on what went wrong and what's next that true celebration is ignored. But acknowledging your success is vital in moving forward with the right energy and attitude.

Remember, what goes around comes around. Not just for bad things, it works for the good stuff too.

10

Mindset Before Mechanics

"Almost every successful person begins with two beliefs: the future can be better than the present, and I have the power to make it so."

David Brooks

Success in any industry or endeavour is the result of strategy, execution and skill. The silent undercurrent running through it all is your mindset. How you think, how you focus and cope with the workload, the pressure and stress.

Your mind is not "set," your mind is like a muscle, and you need to work on it daily to keep it fit. You need to learn how to harness the power to shift your mind, and therefore attention, to a place, thought or direction that will serve you well and not cause you harm.

The topic of the mind is a huge one. In fashion, it is not spoken about a lot, though, in recent times, it is spoken about more than ever. However, I will share with you some of what I know that pertains to supporting you in growing your fashion business through this book.

Secret Ingredients To Success

The fashion industry can be cut-throat. There is a lot of EGOS everywhere you look. Some of it is necessary. A little healthy ego is useful to propel creatives further. However, a lot of it is unhealthy, and knowing how to recognise it and deal with it within yourself and others is key to a healthy mind.

Add to the mental games played inside the fashion industry the fact that, as an entrepreneur, you'll be spending a lot of your time alone, having to work hard, make decisions and solve problems daily.

The two make for a dangerous cocktail, and you have no choice but to consume it. But you have a choice to acknowledge that you are consuming it and be careful how you sip.

A healthy, strong mind will allow you to see everything around you clearly. It allows you to set boundaries (hugely important in an industry that has no rules of its own) for yourself and others, to be decisive and manage the stress of working harder than you ever thought possible. Not to mention the need to be able to manage the entrepreneurial roller coaster of highs and lows that are stronger to feel and even more emotional in the fashion industry.

So you need to first have your mind in check to be able to plan and execute the mechanics. Not the other way around.

Be – Do – Have

One of the most life-changing lessons I recently had from one of my mentors was the idea that, as human beings, we live and do "life" the wrong way around. We operate from a place that has us believing that *if we have* money, success, health, wealth (… whatever you want, insert here), we will then *do -* start a business, exercise, give money to charity, help people. And only then we'll *be* successful, wealthy, healthy, fit, generous, kind, a better human, relaxed.

But, the true and correct model to operate and live from is the opposite - **Be – Do – Have.**

You need to BE a certain type of person first to DO what you want to do and HAVE what you want to have. You need to operate from an identity of the kind of person who does certain things in a particular way and gets to have the desired end results.

Money, fame and success do not happen in isolation and by themselves. They are the end result of taking a series of actions aligned with a certain persona and identity.

Take any big star you know. Be it a fashion designer or sportsman. For the most part, you'll find that if you read up on their journey and how they came to be successful, they visualised, dreamt, and even "knew" all their lives that they were going to be *Big* one day. They visualised BE–ing that person. So they worked hard at their craft, training daily the muscles of their body and mind. Drawing, reading, networking, writing, exercising. Starting small and slowly working towards the bigger goal of having the success, the fame and money that came eventually.

Have you heard of people assuming a false identity and asking, "What would X do if ...?" Sometimes, we all need an alter ego. Assuming the identity of someone we admire and who exemplifies the life and success we want to reach, allows us to gain strength and focus on what we could do in certain situations to move past a challenge.

We all need to do whatever it takes to get what we want.

The Be-Do-Have model is a game-changer.

And so are the following conclusions and revelations I have come to believe are necessary for success.

Powerful Mindshifts

So many people succeed and fail in equal numbers due to "fear." Fear of judgement, failure, change, and self-imposed limiting beliefs. Recognising them and dealing with them one by one is important.

So is knowing that at *"every level there is a new devil."* In other words, the fears never stop. As soon as you deal with one, a new one raises its ugly head.

What do you do? Give up?

No! On the contrary, you face it and keep going and dealing with it. It's part of the journey (and the greater plan, perhaps).

Ego is a necessary evil. We need a little bit to push us farther. To even protect us at times. But use it in good measure and only when necessary.

Kindness is a very underrated quality in the fashion industry. Yet, it is a secret ingredient most successful people will tell you contributed to their success. Kindness offered by others to you and you to others.

The fashion industry is very personal. Things can be absolutely impossible until you meet the right person who is kind enough and "moves mountains" to make the impossible possible.

I can give you countless examples of this from my own working life. Many of them are to do with manufacturing, where the biggest challenges and obstacles often hide.

The key to kindness is giving it with an open heart, willingly and not keeping a score and expecting payback from the same person. What goes around comes around but often not by the people and situations we expect it to. Keep the flow going and detach from exact expectations. Basically, don't try to control the outcome.

Many of the ego-driven problems we face in fashion come from the simple fact that someone somewhere is **not feeling important**. With so many moving parts required to run a fashion brand and business, you will need the involvement of countless people. Many of them are people in professional positions that are important but not seen to be by the outside world. Often and many people in the fashion industry are key contributors, but instead of being acknowledged, they are made to feel like "cogs in a bigger wheel."

Ego driven creatives often forget to recognise and be kind to those, without whom, in all fairness, they will not be able to get to where they are headed. So people get hurt feelings. They act out and lash out. They become difficult and exercise their small powers to create big drama and move attention to themselves.

At every level of the fashion industry, there are people without whose invaluable contribution brands will not reach success, or they'll struggle unnecessarily, in any case, if they tried. Making the smaller people feel important is another secret.

The overlooked, ignored, and overworked assistants in any company often just need small recognition to get the job done, share a shortcut, and influence the final decision. When I was doing my own jewellery brand PR, I was too intimidated to call the big fashion magazine editors. Instead, I called and spoke to the assistant editors. I got friendly with them and found out what was going on, what was coming up, who was working on what and used this information to my advantage later.

In manufacturing, I never visit a factory without a small gift that can be shared with the workers. Biscuits, chocolates… small gestures like this have paid off nicely later. Listen to episode #36 of the Fashion Insider's Podcast and hear how Hayat Rachi, a fashion entrepreneur, grew her brand with the help of her manufacturers. She got better service, top quality products and less manufacturing drama simply because she saw her manufacturer as a partner, not a dispensable stepping stone to success.

Whenever you're in a situation that presents a struggle, look at the people involved (including yourself) and look at who is not feeling like they are heard, seen and recognized. Who needs to feel that they matter and are important? What can you do to change that?

What would X look like if it was simple? When I feel like I am getting caught up in overwhelm, the comparison trap, and the occasional bout of over-perfecting, I often ask myself that question.

Simplifying is always the answer to most challenges, in my experience.

We are wired to strive for more, for better and faster all at the same time. Yet, we often achieve more speed and better results by stripping things to a more basic and manageable state.

Before launching my jewellery brand, I was going round in circles, in my mind, trying to decide what to do. I didn't want to go into clothing where I had abundant amounts of skill, knowledge and experience. Too many things could go wrong, was my reasoning. Leather goods were a preferred option, but I found the high wastage of materials to be an issue. Shoes - too many moving parts and didn't know that much about them. Knitwear - loved the idea and even started designing a collection but was worried about the technicalities of manufacture. Still, it was most appealing to me from various points of consideration I had at the time. And yet, I ended up launching a jewellery brand. Fine jewellery at that.

I had zero knowledge or skills, except love and passion for the product. And it was the simplest thing to do as by chance I met the perfect manufacturer for me and what I had in mind. There was no MOQ involved, and so many other little things that usually create problems were just not present. I had the right people to work with, the right materials on hand, and the right skills. They seemed to (or tried hard) understand me and my ideas, execute my designs, and advise me where I lacked skill and knowledge. The rest I either knew, set on learning or finding the right people who knew more than me.

Easy! OK, it wasn't easy, but it was infinitely easier than driving myself crazy to figure out how to make the impossible possible and give up along the way.

The same happened with launching my podcast. I didn't know anything about audio and podcasts but bought a course that guided me, bought a basic recommended mic, joined a basic easy to use hosting platform, used the basic audio that came with my Mac computer and launched imperfectly. Simple! Could it have been better? Sure! Would it have made a difference? Doubt it!

Done is better than perfect. Taking an imperfect action and moving a step forward is the secret. Every time! You can always perfect later. To be honest, no one but you knows what perfect looks like … unless … there are glaring faults and quality issues that you cannot hide, shouldn't hide and are far from even being "good."

There is a popular book in the world of entrepreneurship called *The E-Myth Revisited* by Michael Gerber. In it, the author explains how to succeed, you need to learn how to **work ON your business and not IN it.** This is very true as far as growing a fashion brand is concerned. Often creative founders are so involved in the minutia like design, sourcing, manufacturing … that they forget there is so much more to running a business.

As the founder, I want you to know that your primary job is to be the visionary, ensure that your vision is translated accurately, and make sure the business doesn't run out of money.

Your brand and business is not an environment where you get to work out your emotional traumas, mental health issues and personal problems. If you bring your ego to work, you need to keep it in check. If you employ and work with others, you need to treat them professionally and respectfully. To this day, the fashion industry still, despite attempts to regulate the employment rules, is an industry where interns, for the most part, remain unpaid and are expected to "show up and put up." There is rarely (if ever) a development plan created for them that would lead to regular employment or simply to enrich their experience and help them further their career later. Many ego-driven brand founders think that an intern or junior employee should be grateful for the opportunity to breathe the same air as the founder. Many genuinely justify not paying fairly (or at all) by thinking that putting the brand's name on a CV later should be enough and the "reward." Yet, they promote their brands as sustainable, ethical and advocate for diversity and equal opportunities.

The fact this still goes on and is "allowed" and tolerated shows that there is still much work to be done by all involved in the fashion industry. It raises the issue of self-worth or, rather, the lack of it amongst all those involved.

The lack of **self-worth** is easily ignored, misunderstood and covered up. It is often at the root of and the cause of many mental health issues. It is tied to how creatives cope with rejection, criticism and haters, which, let's face it, sadly, are all part and parcel of building a successful business in any industry, especially fashion.

Uncoupling your sense of self-worth from any negatively perceived acts and comments is essential to long term survival.

And health and happiness. Realising that *other people's opinions are none of your business* should be a mantra everyone must repeat multiple times daily.

This brings me to the concept of RAC: **Recognise, Acknowledge and Celebrate.** This concept was introduced to me by an Olympian athlete turned business coach, Jason Parker. The idea is that we must stop and take time to recognise how far we have come and celebrate these achievements, no matter how small or large, to grow more as human beings and professionals.

In fashion, we are always living in the future. We are always at least six months ahead of everyone else and often way more than that. We are only in the present to problem solve. Any form of "celebration" is often constructed as part of marketing and for optics and not really for us.

To be able to really RAC it up, you need to slow down and take some time off. To rest and evaluate. Even for a few minutes and do a happy dance.

You need to celebrate in a way that feeds your soul, recharges your internal batteries and gives you joy. The combination of these three create expansion and fuel your imagination and passion. Without it, there is no vision and path to success.

Have you ever heard people say that **"success leaves clues**?" Have you ever wondered what they mean?

Over time, I have come to believe that what they mean is that those who have succeeded have done so because they had a solid plan and the mindset to support it.

Keeping your mind in top condition is an essential everyday job, just like any professional sportsman will look after their body.

The above is just an example of small shifts you can make to help you on your way to building a better fashion brand, a stronger you and a more sustainable business. By doing so, you will come to embody (BE) a person who takes purposeful actions (DO) that steadily take you and your business in the right direction and result in (HAVE) desired outcomes.

Notice how MINDSET comes before mechanics?

(Not) The End For You

"No matter what, people grow. If you choose not to grow, you're staying in a small box with a small mindset. People who win go outside of that box. It's very simple when you look at it."

Kevin Hart

What I want for you more than anything else is to love what you do and do what you love.

I want you to fully experience all that the fashion industry has to offer, overcome the challenges and enjoy the good times. I want to see you own what you are great at, be it creative design or creative thinking, getting featured in magazines, and earning well-deserved money and profits you get to choose what to do with.

Why? Because in today's day and age, you can be creative AND be wildly, commercially successful all in your lifetime.

No matter where you come from, no matter how you express your creativity, and no matter how experienced you are or not, your fashion future can be better if you decide to make the shift.

You get to decide if you are on the inside or on the outside.

No one can have that power over you, and no one can stop you or grant you permission. Only YOU can do that!

At the beginning of this book, I didn't tell you that when I went to do my fashion degree, I rarely attended classes for the first two years. I had to work to support myself, pay my college fees, and save up to attend more classes in my final year. I had no plan how to get into fashion except get into fashion. At times, my choices weren't perfect, and I had a million reasons to feel like an outsider. There were always people who knew less than me and people who knew more than me. I made a choice to believe there was a space and place for all of us inside the fashion industry. If we are IN the industry, we are INSIDERS.

> **In order to become an insider, you need to start thinking like one and not give your power away.**

Fashion Insiders have knowledge and information that sometimes is not so *easily* available to everyone.

Acknowledging that you don't know it all and looking for support and answers through your network of peers, suppliers, and manufacturers is how insiders get to stay on the inside.

Trusting your gut, intuition and all the skills you have accumulated in the course of your life and making use of it all to grow your brand is the insider's mindset.

Using your creativity to sketch ideas, think outside the box, look for solutions to problems outside the fashion industry, and bring them in is how insiders survive. Thinking and acting like an insider will bring you power, prosperity, joy and peace.

> **Surrounding yourself with other creatives, technicians, marketers, and entrepreneurs working on their dreams and doing what they love is how you keep the love of what you do alive.**

And that is how you will build a strong brand and business.

And experience success. One of many.

If you are reading these last few lines, then you already are a Fashion Insider. You officially know more than most people in the industry.

The question now is, what will you do with this knowledge?

The end of this book can be the beginning of something new and big.

This cannot be the end!

This is NOT the end for YOU!

Ready To Become A Fashion Insider?

YOUR INVITATION TO JOIN THE FASHION INSIDERS BUSINESS CLUB.

The Fashion Insiders Business Club is an online community and grow-that-fashion-brand classroom for creatives of all gender and age who are ready to grow their fashion brand and business. No matter what is getting in the way of you making serious money - whether it's shaky confidence, lack of community, knowledge gaps when it comes to design development / manufacturing / pricing / marketing / sales /strategy, or a simply mindset blocks about money (it's okay, we've been there!) - the club has got what you need. It's the perfect next step after reading this book.

We are determined to help you win.

Just like signing up to go and get fit in a gym, the club is a business gym where you get your business fit. It's the place where you go to slay imposter syndrome and get your mindset right; exercise by acquiring new knowledge and skills and meet other like-minded insiders.

Inside the club, we have an entire suite of resources and live weekly coaching dedicated to helping you think like a fashion insider, act as a fashion insider and BE a Fashion Insider.

Need to raise your prices, market your business, or expand your audience? The club offers exclusive training and education to show you exactly how you can grow your business or bring in more revenue.

Looking for your Fashion Insiders' Squad? They're right here, in our thriving community full of ambitious creative entrepreneurs just like you.

So what are you waiting for - come join us at www.fashioninsiders.co/club

About The Author

Dessy Tsolova is a fashion business expert, mentor, coach, and the founder of Fashion Insiders & Co, an educational platform that supports fashion entrepreneurs looking to build fashion brands and create sustainable, profitable businesses.

Her mission is to teach and support creative entrepreneurs in navigating the fashion industry and building purpose-driven brands—without sacrificing their family, health, or sanity in the process.

Dessy started her career working for luxury fashion brands like Burberry, J&M Davidson, Smythson and others and worked her way up from an assistant designer to managing the creative teams and overseeing the entire "idea to product delivery" process. Later on, she spent six years creating one of the first of its kind global online manufacturing platform that helped simplify the process of finding, vetting and working with manufacturers, as well as bring transparency into the fashion supply chain.

When she's not mentoring and coaching, speaking, podcasting, or writing, Dessy loves travelling with her family and exploring new countries and cultures; discovering arts, crafts and meeting creative founders and entrepreneurs.

You can learn more about Dessy, her work and how you can grow your fashion business by visiting www.fashioninsiders.co or by subscribing to the Fashion Insiders & Co podcast and YouTube channel.

Printed in Great Britain
by Amazon

85545513R00129